D0325034

EVANGELISTIC *PREACHING* THAT CONNECTS

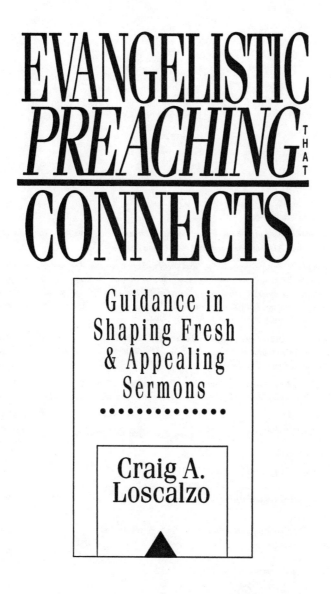

Guidance in
Shaping Fresh
& Appealing
Sermons
•••••••••••••

Craig A.
Loscalzo

IVP

InterVarsity Press
Downers Grove, Illinois

InterVarsity Press® is the book-publishing division of InterVarsity Christian Fellowship®, a student movement active on campus at hundreds of universities, colleges and schools of nursing in the United States of America, and a member movement of the International Fellowship of Evangelical Students. For information about local and regional activities, write Public Relations Dept., InterVarsity Christian Fellowship, 6400 Schroeder Rd., P.O. Box 7895, Madison, WI 53707-7895.

All Scripture quotations, unless otherwise indicated, are from the New Revised Standard Version Bible, copyright © 1989 by the Division of Christian Education of the National Council of the Churches of Christ in the U.S.A., and are used by permission.

Chapter one is adapted from Craig A. Loscalzo, "How Are They to Hear? Evangelism and Proclamation," Review and Expositor 90 (1993): 101-13. Used by permission.

The sermon "The Day of the Lord" is reprinted in chapter six by permission of William H. Willimon.

The sermon "You Can Go Home Again" is reprinted in chapter six by permission of Raymond H. Bailey.

ISBN 0-8308-1863-4

Printed in the United States of America ⊗

Library of Congress Cataloging-in-Publication Data

Loscalzo, Craig A.
    Evangelistic preaching that connects: guidance in shaping fresh &
appealing sermons/Craig A. Loscalzo.
        p.   cm.
    Includes bibliographical references.
    ISBN 0-8308-1863-4 (paper: alk. paper)
    1. Preaching.   2. Evangelistic sermons.   I. Title.
BV4211.2.L674   1995
251—dc20   95-40445
                                                  CIP

| 17 | 16 | 15 | 14 | 13 | 12 | 11 | 10 | 9 | 8 | 7 | 6 | 5 | 4 | 3 | 2 | 1 |
| 09 | 08 | 07 | 06 | 05 | 04 | 03 | 02 | 01 | 00 | 99 | 98 | 97 | 96 | 95 |

*To the students
of the Moscow Theological Institute,
Moscow, Russia, whose lives
exemplify the gospel*

Acknowledgments

The writer of 1 John began his letter (I prefer calling it a sermon) with a declaration:

> We declare to you what was from the beginning, what we have heard, what we have seen with our eyes, what we have looked at and touched with our hands, concerning the word of life—this life was revealed, and we have seen it and testify to it, and declare to you the eternal life that was with the Father and was revealed to us—we declare to you what we have seen and heard so that you also may have fellowship with us; and truly our fellowship is with the Father and with his Son Jesus Christ. We are writing these things so that our joy may be complete. (1:1-4)

What the writer had heard and seen and looked at and touched concerning the Christ of God, he shared with others, to create fellowship *(koinōnia)* and joy. Lives had been transformed through an intimate encounter with Jesus Christ. This passage has formed the foundation for my preaching ministry and my understanding of evangelism. The gospel—that which we have heard and seen and been touched by—we proclaim to others so that they might have fellowship with us, fellowship with God and joy that defies expression. This book grew out of a desire to provide preachers (including myself) help in declaring that good news to others—to those inside and outside the church.

Special thanks goes to the seminary students who were in my summer 1994 course "Evangelistic Preaching." Their feedback to me about the working manuscript proved invaluable for testing ideas and clarifying thought. They affirmed in me the joy of teaching. Thanks also goes to two friends and colleagues, William Willimon and Raymond Bailey, who granted me permission to use their evangelistic sermons in chapter six. I also want to express my gratitude to Rodney Clapp, my editor at InterVarsity Press, for his encouragement in this project and for his guiding it through the publication maze to completion.

In the spring of 1994 I had the privilege to teach preaching among twenty-three students at the Moscow Theological Institute in Moscow, Russia. Their faith in Christ, their understanding of the gospel, their stories of imprisonment for their faith, the way they sang Russian hymns late into the night, their unencumbered embrace of the gospel enlightened my understanding of good news. This book is dedicated to them.

Soli Deo Gloria

1/How Are They to Hear?
Evangelism & Preaching

*W*hat comes to mind when you hear the words *evangelistic preaching?*[1] In an earlier day you might have envisioned a protracted tent meeting, complete with a raspy-voiced preacher ranting about the fires of hell and the demise of God's people because of mixed bathing and women wearing shorts. Evangelistic preaching was defined more by delivery style and less by content. Loudness and sweat marked "good preachin' "! But there was little *evangel* in that kind of preaching. Preaching against the things of the world, the preachers said little, authentically, about the things of God.

I recently received a flyer advertising an upcoming revival meeting in our community. The bold print across the top announced the event: "Fearless Attack Against Sin and Worldliness." The handbill listed what the evangelist would be preaching against:

adultery, divorce and remarriage, marriage annulment, fornication, common-law living, lusting, pimps, hatred, lying, smoking, pride, make-up, certain television programs, alcoholic beverages, suicide, murder, arson, mini skirts, revenge, burglary, rock music, and *the rest that the Bible condemns!* (emphasis added)

And that is only part of the list! Tragically, this kind of harangue illustrates the image people often have of evangelistic preaching. Where is the good news in a sermon that exposes only the ills of the world? Where are the words of hope and redemption in this kind of preaching?

Another image of evangelistic preaching is a modern phenomenon: the TV evangelist. Unfortunately, it is a tainted image in the closing years of the twentieth century. The downfall of several prominent televangelists during the 1980s and the exposure of some other popular—and wealthy—TV preachers by a network news program help portray what society thinks evangelism is all about. Sinclair Lewis embodied these preachers in his fictional character Elmer Gantry. Brother Gantry may well be making a comeback.

Fortunately, these are not the only images that flash across our minds when we hear someone mention evangelistic preaching. In any conversation about contemporary evangelism, someone inevitably mentions Billy Graham. With his well-organized metropolitan crusades, Graham is considered by many to be the quintessential model of evangelistic preaching in the second half of the twentieth century. A man of impeccable character, he has held both the banner and the demands of evangelistic preaching high. In an article in *Christianity Today* Graham challenged preachers to communicate the gospel by a holy life. "Our world today," he noted, "is looking primarily for men and women of integrity, communicators who back up their ministry with their lives."[2] For more than forty years Graham has exemplified the evangelist whose life reflects the good news he preaches.

Although these pictures portray the examples most visible to society, they don't describe the evangelistic preaching most of us do. Few of us are television evangelists, nor do we regularly preach in community-wide evangelistic campaigns. Many evangelical ministers associate evangelism and preaching with the still-popular church revival, typically held in the fall or spring of the year. Whereas particular expectations about revival meetings are different in various parts of the country, people universally consider evangelistic preaching the key element.

Evangelism is also a part of the preaching task of pastors in local congregations. However, two extremes often characterize the place of evangelistic preaching in this setting: every sermon is preached for the benefit of unchurched persons who happen to be visiting the congregation, or no sermon is ever preached for the benefit of unchurched visitors. Hopefully most pastors find their evangelistic preaching falling somewhere between these two extremes.

All preachers should seriously consider the role evangelistic preaching has in their ministry, and this book is designed to help them do that. This introductory chapter will deal with several overarching issues related to evangelism and proclamation.

First we will consider the contribution human beings make to the evangelistic enterprise. Does successful evangelism reside in the effectiveness of the evangelist? Or is evangelism wholly a divine venture?

Then we will look at contemporary contexts, the stage on which evangelism takes place. Preaching never happens in a vacuum. Before we compose evangelistic sermons, we had better take stock of the world in which we live, or our efforts may never find ears to hear.

After that we will focus attention on several communication concerns that preachers must consider. The soundest theology poorly communicated will never gain a hearing.

Finally, we will discuss the persuasive elements of evangelistic preaching. The term *persuasion* often conjures up negative images. But persuasion need not be suspect.

With these broad issues of evangelism and proclamation as a foundation, the balance of the book will focus on evangelistic preaching that connects.

An Incarnational Model for Evangelism and Preaching

I get a bit nervous when I hear some ministers talk about evangelism: "I led three people to the Lord last week," or "He's a real soul-winner." My anxiety comes from the implication of these comments. Unwittingly they give credit to the minister's initiative, prowess and zeal as an evangelist. These accounts make it sound as if the impetus for evangelism rests in the lap of the person. That may be the reason many laypeople cower at the mention of the word. Is it possible that ministers make evangelism the "E-word" for church members because they speak of it in terms of the evangelist's success?

Laypeople often feel inadequate when it comes to evangelism. They are frequently dubious of their ability to speak to others about their faith. They falsely assume that evangelism requires the ability to quote vast amounts of Scripture. Since they don't have the Bible memorized, they feel inadequate to share their faith. They will surely avoid evangelism if the basis for success lies in their abilities, their biblical knowledge or their skill as evangelists. Ministers may unintentionally create a negative environment for evangelism in the church by emphasizing our "success stories." No doubt, the Bible clearly indicates the importance of human participation in evangelization (Mt 28:19-20; Rom 10). To overemphasize the human initiative, however, is to succumb to a subtle form of humanism.

To guard against such, I suggest we use the Incarnation—with a capital *I*—as the key to understanding the role we as human beings play in evangelism. The doctrine of the Incarnation describes the mystery of God becoming flesh, taking on human form and experiencing life as a person (Jn 1:14). In the wisdom of God, which so often appears to us as mystery, God chose to experience humanity fully. Jesus Christ, God incarnate, was both fully human and fully divine. In Christ, God experienced what it means to be human (2 Cor 5:19). He felt joy, hardship, temptation, pain, anxiety, frustration and humiliation. Jesus Christ was also fully divine. In Jesus Christ we see, though difficult to comprehend fully, perfect humanity and divinity. Jesus Christ was God/human.

In a way, ministry models the Incarnation. All ministry has a twofold dimension. It is incarnation with a little *i:* God—the divine side of the incarnation equation—works through our gifts, personalties, experiences and training—the human side of the incarnation equation. Though we do not understand the reason, God chose to work in the world through his own people, the church.

That should not surprise us, for God foreshadowed that plan in the life of Jesus Christ. God worked in the world through his own Son. Jesus, with his life and ministry, brought the presence of God from heaven to earth. The Incarnation reminds us that God is not a distant landlord, uninterested in the world. In Jesus Christ, God became a human player in human history. When we minister on behalf of Jesus Christ, we, through the power of the Holy Spirit, continue what God began in him (Jn 20:21).

Where do we see evidence of this divine-human partnership in our ministry? Take a typical part of a pastor's ministry: hospital visitation. What happens when we go to the hospital and hold the hand of a sick church member, and he or she is comforted? Someone might say that the caring touch and compassion of another human being comforts the patient; you don't have to be a Christian to comfort someone. An incarnational understanding of ministry, however, will not let us stop the explanation there. We believe that we mediate the presence of God. We don't understand how it takes place, but God's Holy Spirit comforts the patient through our presence (Mt 18:20), a divine-human encounter. I have no doubt that God can and does comfort hospital patients when no person is present. But when we involve ourselves in authentic ministry, we can never assume that we alone are mediators of any blessing. The model of the Incarnation demands that.

Evangelism, being an aspect of ministry, demonstrates this divine-human character. Evangelism begins with, is sustained by and ultimately ends with God. *We* don't convert people. *We* don't "win" anyone to the Lord. *We* don't make Christians. God does. Therefore evangelism is a divine task, though it has a human dimension. We are workers *with* God (1 Cor 3:9); God chooses to work through the gifts of people. We don't merely report events that took place two thousand years ago. We are recipients of the gospel and heralds of good news that is available now. We have experienced and celebrate God's grace, and we long for others to join our celebration.

This idea models D. T. Niles's definition of evangelism as one beggar telling another beggar where to find bread. As persons respond to the good news, lives are changed, individuals experience personal faith in Jesus Christ as Lord and Savior, and they become active members of the church, participants in God's kingdom and obedient as servants in the world. We participate with God in spreading the gospel of Jesus Christ, an incarnational model of evangelism.

Preaching is a divine-human endeavor.[3] Think of a time when a church member leaving a worship service has mentioned how the sermon spoke to her particular problem, or a churchwide fellowship meal when a person commented on how a sermon helped meet a need in his life. As you recall the sermon, you wonder how he could have heard what he heard, how she could have received the help she received, how they felt as comforted as they did. As you think about the sermon, you don't remember saying anything directly related to his or her situation. Is it just a coincidence that the sermon was a word they needed to hear? I think not. In the mystery of the divine-human encounter that takes place when a community of faith gathers to worship, God takes our words and enables them to communicate the Word.

The Holy Spirit works with the preacher as sermons are prayed about, planned, composed and preached. The Holy Spirit also works in the lives of our hearers. Sunday after Sunday, a faith community gathers to encounter the presence of God. People come to church to sing the hymns, to pray the prayers, to read the Scriptures, to listen for the Word of God. They don't come to hear the choir sing, nor do they come to hear us preach. They come to meet God, to experience God's presence, to feel God's comfort, to offer to God a word of thanksgiving.

Our preaching is incarnational. We put into it our best efforts of exegesis as we interpret biblical texts, our best pastoral skills as we seek to minister to our people through preaching, our best rhetorical skills for composing a sermon that speaks to life situations and needs of the gathered congregation. If we stop there, however, our words are but "a noisy gong or a clanging cymbal" (1 Cor 13:1). It is when God imbues our words that authentic Christian preaching takes place. Christian preaching, as defined by Phillips Brooks, is the bringing of "truth through personality."[4]

What, then, is the role of the Holy Spirit in evangelism and preaching? The Holy Spirit works in the life of the preacher and in the lives of hearers. As a group of people gathers to hear the Word proclaimed, God is already working in their midst. In every gathering there are probably those who have never responded in any way to the gospel. The illuminating power of the Holy Spirit enables people to understand truth as it is proclaimed. The Holy Spirit convicts of sin, calls people to Christ and effects regeneration.[5] We recall Paul's words:

For, "Everyone who calls on the name of the Lord shall be

saved." But how are they to call on one in whom they have not believed? And how are they to believe in one of whom they have never heard? And how are they to hear without someone to proclaim him? (Rom 10:13-14)

Contemporary Contexts for Evangelism and Preaching

Today's world is strange and complex. Characterized by pluralism, diversity, the proliferation of and dependence on technology, multiculturalism, economic interdependence between nations, a widening gap between the rich and the poor (both individuals and nations), a rapidly growing concern for the demise of inner cities and a new appreciation for freedom and human dignity, this world is the context for our evangelism and preaching.[6] It is a world too enigmatic for shallow analysis, too complex for quick fixes and too perplexing for religious clichés. Many old rules for understanding the world must be modified or totally transformed. Envisioning contemporary contexts requires preachers to broaden their horizons so that their preaching has an impact on this world.

Preaching is a discipline performed by general practitioners. Preachers must be students of the Bible, theology, church history, pastoral care and counseling. They must also be students of human nature, sociology, political science and cultural trends (just to name a few). The stage on which we preach is the world; for us to preach effectively, we must understand the present world and envision the future world into which we and our hearers are moving. To do any less would be to violate the nature of the evangelistic task of taking good news to the whole world.

Envisioning contexts for evangelism and preaching requires that we identify and overcome some contemporary obstacles. A common thread running through surveys of religious belief in the United States, for example, is that Americans are generally religious, claim to believe in God and, to a lesser extent, claim that America is a Christian nation. These claims, though on the surface sounding positive and reassuring, often create obstacles to our evangelistic endeavors. "Religious people" have little desire to hear the gospel proclaimed, because they think they are already religious enough.

It is difficult to say where these views come from or why Americans view themselves as a religious nation. I suspect that a subtle and dangerous civil religion, a form of humanism, has perpetrated the illusion. The god invoked along with Mom, apple pie, baseball and Fourth of July parades is not necessarily the God of the Bible. The god to which many Americans dedicate their allegiance is a god of nationalism, wrapped in the flag and worshiped for convenience and selfishness. Many Americans have confused patriotism with biblical theology.

Do not misunderstand me. I served as a U.S. Air Force missile specialist in Thailand during the Vietnam War. I am grateful to live in America; I enjoy the freedoms that are ours. We must remember, however, that God is not an American, and America is not God's chosen people. That distinction belongs to the church, the *ekklēsia* (1 Pet 2:9-10). The church, not America, is the new Israel. The New Testament and the claims of Christ's gospel stand over against any nationalistic understanding of the Christian faith.

I agree, to an extent, with Donald Posterski when he says, "In the future, we can expect increasing anti-Christian sentiment toward the claims of Christ and toward the people who hold firmly to the Lord's views."[7] It may be better, however, to observe that apathy or indifference toward Christ's claims may be more real and detrimental than any increase in anti-Christian sentiment.

The first step in overcoming the obstacles of pseudo-Christianity is to recognize them. Then we must not assume that our hearers agree with our basic presuppositions about the faith. Evangelism and proclamation begin with the assumption that some hearers, whether on a typical Sunday morning or during special services, have no biblical or theological basis for understanding any truth claims made by the gospel. In fact, many people sitting in the pews lack familiarity with the stories, images and characters of our faith. Our evangelistic preaching cannot assume that all our hearers understand allusions to Abraham's faith, David's sin and repentance, or the elder brother's anger over the party thrown for his younger and prodigal sibling.

Evangelistic preaching must begin with the premise that some hearers have absolutely no background for the faith and must be addressed from that presupposition. A biblical example is to compare the preaching of the apostle Paul to Jews in the synagogue and his preaching at the Areopagus in Acts 17. He knew that his Gentile hearers had no foundation in the faith of Israel, so he began his sermon by speaking to their immediate understanding.

As we face the diversity and pluralism present in the world, another obstacle is the assumption that our culture and worldview is the only one. Contemporary contexts require preachers to move beyond provincial understandings; ministers who intentionally cultivate a worldview will be the most effective gospel preachers.

Those of us who are from the South sometimes incorporate Southern culture into our Christianity. Lottie Moon, one of the first Southern Baptist women missionaries sent to China, was criticized for not requiring the Chinese to dress and act like Americans. In fact, when she decided to wear local dress and participate in Chinese customs, denominational leaders in the United States reprimanded her.[8]

For a contemporary example, Southern Baptists (of whom I am one) are known for prohibiting dancing. They are so known for this practice that many probably think that Baptist distinctives are no smoking, no drinking and *no dancing*. Some

Southern Baptists become indignant when they find out that other Baptists have no problem at all with dancing. Indeed, in some parts of the world dance is an integral part of Christian worship. But many of us assume that all Christians should follow our example, even when the prohibition (such as no dancing) is more cultural than theological. In light of contemporary contexts, we must be careful not to presume, as part of our evangelistic message, that our cultural mores are binding on others. The difficulty for us will be to see the universality of the good news through our particular cultural lenses.

Because the world is rapidly changing, we must be ready to change our evangelistic methods and strategies. This doesn't mean that we compromise the gospel for the sake of not offending someone or that we dilute the demands of the gospel because it speaks against certain cultural practices. What it does mean is that we seek methods of proclamation and evangelism that people will hear and to which they will respond. The church often clings to the myth that what has worked before will work now. This assumption may prevent the church from effectively speaking to a complex and changing world.

For example, confrontational forms of evangelism were at one time frequently used by evangelicals. I once heard an evangelist say that every Christian should witness to every person they meet: "Confront them with the gospel and call them to repentance right then and there!" But my experience with many Asian seminary students and Asian friends tells me that in their culture a direct, frontal approach to introducing someone to Christ would be considered so rude that the hearers would not respond to the gospel; they would not be able to get beyond the rudeness of the evangelist.

"Confrontational styles of witnessing were never popular, but today they are considered offensive," wrote Posterski.[9] "We're going to get nowhere fast," wrote Alfred Krass, "by laying guilt trips on middle-class North American Christians."[10] Contemporary writers on evangelism have just as much zeal as confrontational evangelists, but they promote an evangelism that grows out of relationships.

Some confrontational approaches to evangelism are based on the assumption that we must prove the veracity of Jesus Christ. Richard Armstrong objects to such an approach: "I came to realize that our task as Christian witnesses is not to prove that Jesus Christ is the son of God. That we can never do. Our role as witnesses is to show by the way we speak and act that we really *believe* he is. That, *by God's grace,* we can do!"[11] As we seek to proclaim good news to future generations we must explore new methods and strategies so that people hear the "old, old story."

I must sound a warning here. In an attempt to be contemporary and speak to various cultures, many preachers and churches go off the deep end. I was amused by Martin Marty's column in *The Christian Century* about churches promoting "market-driven religion."[12] He wrote about a church whose Sunday worship consists of "good humor, light rock, comedy sketches," as well as "poignant personal stories and rituals that replace alleluias with 'Yeeeah!' 'Unbelieeevable!' 'Awwwwesome!' " The pastor of the church doesn't want to offend anyone, for when a church is market-driven the customer is always right. If a person wants to be baptized by immersion, that's fine; if by sprinkling, no problem. Marty quoted the pastor as saying, "We'll backflip someone into the pool if that's what they really want. . . . We don't want baptism to become a barrier that would keep anyone from Christianity." Marty was lamenting a form of Christianity that gives the consumers what they want at the cost of authentic faith. His closing remark is noteworthy: "I'll just keep my fingers crossed about this 21st-century form of faith and try to leap right past it to the 22nd century, with more hope."

Myriad books have been published in recent years dealing

with church marketing and growth. George Barna, for one, has offered some important insights for understanding the baby boomer and baby buster generations and how churches can reach out to them.[13] Many ministers, desperately looking for ways to reach younger people, see methods such as Barna's as answers to prayer. I sound a strong word of caution here. Marketing the church must be done with integrity and authenticity. I hear ministers talking about all the latest ways they "meet the needs of the boomers." The real danger in these methods is that evangelism turns into a smorgasbord approach. Church becomes a cafeteria line where people pick and choose parts of the gospel that fit their lifestyle. The danger becomes that we will dilute the scandal of the gospel in order to be evangelistically successful. But because the gospel is sometimes hard to hear, evangelism cannot be consumer-driven.

Envisioning contemporary contexts for evangelism and proclamation requires ministers to find creative yet authentic ways to speak to an ever-changing, ever-complex world. Remember, God is also God of the future. We don't step into the unknown alone.

Faith Comes from Hearing

Since, as Paul wrote, faith does come from hearing, our task as proclaimers of the gospel is to be heard. An abiding principle for preachers is that understanding is always at the ear of the hearer, not at the mouth of the speaker. No matter how well we understand the gospel, even if our understanding is clearer than that of any other pastor, evangelist or theologian, if we are unable to communicate that insight to people, our knowledge is of no use. We must keep our hearers in mind whenever we preach, for they are the recipients of our preaching efforts. This is especially important when it comes to evangelism and preaching.

Our assumption for preaching evangelistic sermons is some

among our hearers have never responded to Jesus Christ and his message of the inauguration of the reign of God. We want them to hear the gospel preached, to have an understanding of the message they hear and to have a chance to respond appropriately to that message. We often tragically assume that they are familiar with the language we use in church.

I heard an evangelist use the following refrain throughout a revival sermon: "If you've never been washed in the blood of the Lamb, then you have a decision to make tonight." None of us would argue with the basic theological truth of that assertion. Do you realize, though, what a person has to know to comprehend that statement? It presumes that the listeners understand the sacrificial system of Israel, the role of blood in that sacrifice and the idea of an unblemished lamb, to name the more obvious facets. If a person has never been to church or been exposed to church language, how can he or she possibly comprehend the meaning of such a statement? Avoiding the use of theological jargon—the language of Zion—in evangelistic sermons will help less knowledgeable hearers understand the gospel message.

Theological terms such as *sanctified, justified, expiation, propitiation, righteousness* and *sin* are often misunderstood by uninformed hearers. These words may be appropriate and necessary when theologians speak to theologians. However, when preachers speak to people, technical theological language should be translated into words all listeners can understand. When medical doctors rattle off a technical term describing our condition, we become unnerved. "Give it to me in English, Doc" is a common response. Hearers can react to the gospel only when they understand what they hear. Jesus did not use theological language when he preached. He spoke in terms that were understood and grasped by the people—an excellent model for evangelistic preaching.

A similar concern is that preachers should model the inclusiveness of the gospel in their preaching. We believe that the gospel is for all people; our language and our choice of illustrative material should model that. Beyond avoiding theological jargon, the language of evangelistic sermons should be appropriate for your particular group of hearers. Preaching to a rural congregation may require very different choices of words and images from those used in preaching to an urban church. Make sure that the language you use fits the particular group of hearers.

The same advice is true for illustrative material. Allusions to Shakespeare, classic films or lyrics of contemporary songs may speak clearly to one congregation but go totally over the heads of another. Because we want our hearers to see that the good news includes them, we can model that by including them in the sermon. Our choice of language and sermonic material is a beginning point for making that happen.

We reveal our attitude toward people by our language. Therefore the language we use when we preach should be inclusive. The gospel demands no less. All people should *explicitly* know that they are included when we preach: men, women, children, youth, senior adults, single adults, married people, divorced people, people with disabilities—everyone. Preaching that uses only masculine pronouns and always refers to people as "men" excludes women in the congregation. We want people, especially unchurched people, to hear that the good news includes them. If children are in the congregation, choose words they will understand; if you don't, you exclude them from hearing the gospel. Young people have their own vocabulary. Do you know any of their words? Will they want to listen to you when you preach because they sense that you have been sensitive to their presence? Senior adults will not understand some slang used by baby boomers. "CD" probably means "certificate of deposit" for senior adults but "compact disc" for younger hearers. Help all your hearers know what you mean by clarifying the use of popular terms such as *CD, MTV* and *ASAP.*

Inclusive language is language that includes rather than excludes, invites rather then repels, accepts rather than rejects. The very nature of the gospel of Jesus Christ includes all who will respond.

Evangelistic sermons, like all preaching, should be interesting, vibrant and life-situational. The best biblical insights preached in a dull, boring way are not heard, and how shall they believe if they do not hear? *Interesting* doesn't mean entertaining. *Interesting* means touching the nerve of your hearers where they live and move and have their being. People listen when they perceive that the topic has import for their lives.

This is particularly crucial when it comes to evangelistic preaching, because many nonbelievers are skeptical of organized religion. They don't feel that the church is relevant. They have not seen evidence that the church really speaks to issues facing a complex society. Many nonbelievers have been exposed to preaching that was nebulous and esoteric, was difficult to understand and made no sense.

Through interesting sermons, the Bible addresses the needs of real people leading real lives. The longing for meaning and acceptance and the need to make sense out of life are addressed by the gospel. The evangel speaks to the pain of loneliness and the feeling of isolation from God and others. Sin shackles people's lives. Addictions to relationships, possessions and success are sins that can be transformed by the grace of Jesus Christ. Abusive behaviors that break apart families are addressed by the gospel: the Bible is replete with stories about real families, broken families that needed God's grace and love.

Is it possible that Zacchaeus was so overwhelmed by isolation from his people and God that he climbed a tree just to get a glimpse of Jesus? Jesus went to his home, and Zacchaeus was visibly changed. The Bible tells of a dysfunctional family whose younger son wanted what was coming to him, even before his father died, and whose older son could not share in his father's joy. When Jesus told the story of the prodigal son, people sat up and listened, especially those who had children, children who did not always think and act like parents expect children to act. Address people where they hurt and struggle, and your sermons will be interesting.

Another way to create interesting sermons is to avoid propositional preaching. Such proclamation often talks *about* the gospel. The preacher gleans certain theological ideas from a biblical text, states the ideas as propositions, then sets out to prove or explain why the precepts are true. Posterski rightly asserts, "There is a significant difference between talking about God and telling God's truth. Witnessing effectively is not just dispensing information."[14] There is a difference between preaching *about* Christ crucified and preaching Christ crucified. The former provides the hearers with more information; the latter transforms the hearers with the power of the gospel.

Stereotypically, propositional preaching concentrates on points to be made, concepts to be learned, ideas to be accepted; the focus is on the dissemination of information. It assumes that people's behavior will change if they have the correct knowledge. Transformational preaching focuses on the intersection between the gospel and the hearer's life situation. Propositional preaching answers the question "What is this text about?" Transformational preaching answers the question "How will my life be different if I take this text seriously?"

Transformational preaching relies heavily on the use of stories and examples from life situations. It enables the hearers to see themselves in the stories of Scripture, to be confronted by the Christ who is revealed in the pages of the Bible, to be changed. One can know all about Jesus and still live the same. But to meet Jesus face-to-face in a sermon, one's life is never the same again. To be sure, sermons must be based on sound biblical theology, but the theology is only a means to an end.

The end is to encounter the risen Christ.

Persuasion and Evangelistic Preaching

People continually try to persuade other people to do something. Advertisers try to persuade us to buy their products. Doctors try to persuade us to be more health conscious. When my son asks, "Dad, if I mow the grass, will you give me some money so I can go to the movies?" he is using a form of persuasive communication. When Paul and Silas said, "Believe on the Lord Jesus, and you will be saved" (Acts 16:31), they were using persuasive speech. Persuasion is

☐ "a communication process in which the communicator seeks to elicit a desired response."[15]

☐ "that activity in which speaker and listener are conjoined and in which the speaker consciously attempts to influence the behavior of the listener by transmitting audible and visible symbolic cues."[16]

☐ "communicative behavior that has as its purpose the changing, modification, or shaping of the responses (attitudes or behavior) of the receivers."[17]

Evangelistic preaching is persuasive preaching: we seek a desired response, and we consciously attempt to influence the attitudes and behaviors of our listeners. That should not surprise us. The gospel itself is inherently persuasive. Its message intends to evoke changes in people's attitudes and to elicit transformation of their behaviors (2 Cor 5:17). Motivated by our love for people, we want to persuade them to accept the gift of new life in Jesus Christ. The gospel has reached deep inside us, convicted us of our sin, has healed our brokenness and made us whole persons in Jesus Christ. The gospel has set us on a lifetime pilgrimage of walking with Christ. We desperately want others to experience this salvation. We want to persuade them to receive God's offer of life. Persuasive preaching aims at that end.

We must remember two crucial things about persuasive preaching. First, we are earthen vessels used by the Holy Spirit. Our preaching must never get in God's way. Second, persuasion *never* means coercion. When it comes to evangelistic preaching, the end never justifies the means. Lewis Drummond stated the issue well: "Any form of evangelism that resorts to the manipulation of people, regardless of the motive, is unworthy of the gospel."[18] The way we proclaim the gospel, how we seek to persuade people to respond to the gospel, must be in line with the character of the gospel. Jesus tried to persuade all who listened to respond to his message, but he never coerced or manipulated anyone into the kingdom.

What are some questionable methods in persuasive preaching?[19] One is the use of scare tactics. Fear is a volatile emotion. People respond to certain requests when frightened, though often involuntarily. Intentionally scaring people to get them to respond to the gospel is manipulation. Frightening people for the sake of good news is oxymoronic. One cannot find scare tactics as a method of evangelism in the New Testament. Authentically speaking about the consequences of rejecting the gospel can be done without intentionally frightening people.

It is also unethical to take advantage of certain situations. An example is using a funeral as an opportunity to "get somebody saved." Grief is a powerful emotion. People will do or say anything when they experience the death of a loved one. To use their weakened state as an evangelistic occasion is opportunistic. The purpose of the funeral sermon is to comfort the bereaved. Sharing our witness about God's available grace to sustain us in times of deep pain and loss is most appropriate. Speaking about Christ's victory over death and the grave is absolutely fitting. Go ahead and share a message of good news. If there are people at the funeral who have never responded to Christ's offer of new life, they will hear that. Then, after they have had a chance for their pain to subside, make follow-up visits. In this process your care and concern offers a persuasive witness for them to accept God's love in Jesus Christ. Such an approach, in the spirit of agape (unconditional love), honors the essence of the gospel.

Emotionalism is another example of a questionable method of persuasive preaching. I differentiate between an authentic appeal to emotions in preaching and emotionalism. God created us beings with intellect and emotions. We respond to life holistically through both. Ralph Lewis states, "There are strong emotional factors in persuasion. While logic is concerned primarily with information, persuasive action is closely linked to emotion."[20] To share a sad personal story may be extremely appropriate. Helping people to remember a joyful time in their lives is a fitting appeal to emotion. Humor is a wonderfully effective emotion for preaching. People respond to "sincere emotional appeals based upon reality, human experience, good sense and appropriateness."[21] It makes sermons lifelike. However, to end a sermon with the proverbial "dying dog story" so that people will flood the aisles during the invitation is coercive.

Effective persuasive preaching appeals to both the intellect and the emotions, the listener's mind and will. People are persuaded to action by logical reasoning, by examples, by stories and by hearing how the good news intersects their daily life situations. Through effective evangelistic preaching people are persuaded to experience new life in Christ.

Summing Up
In a world characterized by pluralism, diversity, dependence on technology and multiculturalism, the challenges for spreading the gospel of Jesus Christ are immense. Evangelistic preaching requires preachers, imaginatively and creatively, to preach sermons that bring the story of God's love to present and future generations. "How are they to hear without someone to proclaim him?" (Rom 10:14).

2/Who's Afraid of the Big Bad Wolf? Toward a Theology for Evangelistic Preaching

*I*n one version of the folktale "The Three Little Pigs," the cute curly-tailed heroes (beauty *is* in the eye of the beholder), dressed as young schoolchildren, are ready to head off to their first day of class. But they are terrorized by a voracious wolf banging on their door and chanting, "Little pigs, little pigs, let me come in!"

The pigs' response is immediate and predictable: "Not by the hair on our chinny, chin, chins!"

"Then I'll huff and I'll puff and I'll *bloooow* your house in!" replies the determined intruder.

Of course, since this is a fairy tale, the pigs defeat their enemy through creative ingenuity. The wolf is run off, never to harass the pigs again; and now it is their turn to sing refrains: "Who's afraid of the big bad wolf, the big bad wolf, the big bad wolf? Who's afraid of the big bad wolf?" The obvious answer to the rhetorical question is "nobody." The wolf has been chased far into the next county to badger some other unsuspecting souls, but it is not going to bother the pigs again—at least for a while.

In the previous chapter, I mentioned the fear that many laypersons have when they hear the word *evangelism*. I'm not sure I understand all the reasons for it, but my suspicion is that many ministers, whatever their denominational affiliation, also treat evangelism with the same kind of fear and trepidation that the pigs had when they shuddered before the wolf. This fear may be grounded in a perceived lack of expertise, as if evangelism were a matter of cooking: if the steps to the recipe are followed correctly, a product emerges from the oven that is good for food and a delight to the eyes. A profusion of five-easy-steps-to-evangelism books grace Christian bookstores' shelves, promising effective evangelistic results. Perhaps the fear of not knowing the right way to go about evangelism is a provoked anxiety. Nevertheless, many ministers avoid evangelistic preaching, or any kind of evangelism for that matter, because they're afraid they don't know how to do it.

Another element may be the unrelenting fear of failure pervading our society. An advertisement for a national banking firm claims that "Americans want to succeed, not just survive." Nobody wants to be a failure, especially in religious work. Failure becomes synonymous with a lack of conviction or a shortage of faith. Since evangelism is often defined as "getting someone saved," the results seem easily measured. If someone "got saved," you were successful; if no one "got saved," you failed. Who wants to fail? "Rather than risk failure, I'll make a hospital visit" goes the logic. "Can't go wrong visiting the hospital."

Perhaps the fear of offending someone keeps us hiding from evangelism. After all, we are progressive Christians—some more conservatively progressive than others, but progressive nonetheless. We have been offended by well-meaning (giving them the benefit of the doubt), zealous "missionaries" from some religious group knocking at our door at the most inopportune time, telling us that all we believe, all we have based our lives on, all that matters to us when it comes to God-things is wrong. And then they have the gall to tell us that they hold *the truth* we need. "The audacity," we mutter under our breath. "Who do they think they are?" we seethe. "No thank you!" we curtly reply. "We don't need any *truth* today!" As we walk away from the door, the slam still echoing in our ears, we vow never to be so offensive with *our* faith. Later, someone mentions evangelism, perhaps at a minister's conference, and our immediate word association is *offensive*. We pull out a scrap of paper and make a note that we have to stop and see someone in the hospital on the way home.

Being labeled narrow-minded may create an anxiety about evangelism. We ministers, like all people, want people to think well of us. We work hard to be accepted, to be liked, to be appreciated. No matter the setting—the Monday ministers' meeting, a gathering of friends at a party, a softball team get-together—when someone is labeled narrow-minded, the tacit understanding is that they are not liked very much, and that's an understatement.

Who likes someone who is unwilling to look at new ideas? Think about the last time you looked forward to spending an afternoon with a person who demonstrated a rigidity toward the views of others or a lack of tolerance for other people's perspectives. We avoid people like that as though they had the plague. They are just not pleasant to be around. They usually make us mad every time they open their mouths. And evangelists are often labeled narrow-minded.

No wonder we avoid evangelistic preaching. We don't want to be considered evangelists—not if it means being labeled close-minded. After all, we pursued years of education, through university and seminary studies, to broaden our outlook, to free us from the shackles of provincialism, to open the vistas of new horizons, to shed our unhealthy biases. The apostle Paul's admonition to stand firm and not to submit again to a yoke of slavery (Gal 5:1) sounds to us a clarion call for receptivity to new ideas. When evangelism becomes synonymous with an insular mindset, we should avoid it like the little pigs avoided the wolf.

The fears of evangelism mentioned here, like most worries, have some measure of validity. However, like fear of the dark, when we turn the light on, the danger is narrowed down to size. Anxiety toward evangelism can be placed in proper perspective. Hence, the fear of not knowing how effectively to do evangelistic ministry can be overcome by learning what evangelism really is and what it is not. Like other aspects of ministry, authentic methods of evangelism can be learned.

However, the danger for preachers is to succumb to the fallacy of the "power of techniques."[1] Alan Walker made the point well when he observed that the task of conversion is God's not ours: "A preacher can be an instrument in God's hands to persuade others to surrender to Christ, to open their lives to the Holy Spirit, to take the vital, inescapable step of allowing Christ to enter the human heart and cause the miracle of conversion."[2] The idea for us to grasp is that we can learn ways to be effective evangelistically, but authentic evangelism transcends any particular method.

Again, the fear of failing at evangelism can be overcome by rightly understanding the theological motivation for evangelistic ministry. Particularly, success is never a motive for any kind of ministry. Our call to ministry demands a commitment of fidelity to the task. If our faithfulness yields results that can be labeled successful, fine. Our goal requires faithfulness to our call, leaving the results to the one we serve. Our ministry is a means to God's end.

The fear of being offensive and of being labeled narrow-minded is a real fear, for some evangelists are offensive and narrow-minded—sometimes by intentional design. The tragedy is that, whereas the gospel represents a "stumbling block" to some and "foolishness" to others, when the evangelist himself or herself becomes the stumbling block or the fool, the hearers may never have the opportunity to encounter the scandal of the gospel. In a society where relativism—the idea that truth is not an absolute but is merely related to the persons or groups holding it—commonly pervades, making claims about the unique significance of the work of Christ might be offensive to some and sound close-minded to others.

Perhaps these fears will subside when we recognize that the content of our message, the substance of this gospel, is *good news*. What we have is *good news!* Good news is easy to share, open-mindedly and respectfully. In a culture inundated with bad news on every side, what a welcome breath of fresh air your *news* will be. "Do not be afraid," said the angel, "for see—I am bringing you *good news* of great joy for all the people" (Lk 2:10; emphasis added).

What, Exactly, Is This Good News?

In church circles we hear the word *gospel* thrown around as though everybody knows exactly what it means. What is this *good news?* What do the writers of New Testament convey when they use the term *euangelion* (gospel)? For years a starting point for such discussions has been C. H. Dodd's pivotal work *The Apostolic Preaching and Its Developments.*[3] In it he drew a line between what he saw as two strands of preaching in the New Testament, a distinction that he believed was drawn by the writers of the New Testament themselves. This two-foci emphasis was preaching whose content was *kērygma* and preaching that focused on *didachē.*

Kērygma was the salvific message proclaimed to those who had not yet come to faith in Jesus Christ as God's anointed one. In other words, *kērygma* was the message rooted in the historical events about Jesus of Nazareth, primarily concerning his death, resurrection and exaltation. These events were the heart of *euangelion. Didachē,* on the other hand, was catechetical preaching and ethical instruction designed to guide and instruct believers in the faith so as to uplift and strengthen their believing communities. In the most basic sense, then, *kērygma* was preaching for conversion, and *didachē* was preaching to instruct those who had been converted.

The dichotomy drawn by Dodd between *kērygma* and *didachē* seems too radical. My own reading of the New Testament does not warrant such a strict line of demarcation between the strands of preaching. The border between *kērygma* and *didachē* seems to be grayer than Dodd concluded.[4] Nevertheless, Dodd did name characteristics or elements of the *kērygma* that help us see the nature of evangelistic preaching within the New Testament; hence enabling us to come to a sound understanding of the good news.

Dodd presented two major summaries of the *kērygma*. One summary included fragments of early Christian preaching located in Paul's epistles:

The prophecies [of the Old Testament] are fulfilled, and the new Age is inaugurated by the coming of Christ.

He was born of the seed of David.

He died according to the Scriptures, to deliver us out of the present evil age.

He was buried.

He rose on the third day according to the Scriptures.

He is exalted at the right hand of God, as Son of God and Lord of [the] quick and dead.

He will come again as Judge and Saviour of [humankind].[5]

Dodd's second summary illustrated the *kērygma* of the Jerusalem church presented by Luke in the first four sermons of Peter in the book of Acts:

First, the age of fulfillment has dawned.

Secondly, this has taken place through the ministry, death, and resurrection of Jesus. . . .

Thirdly, by virtue of the resurrection, Jesus has been exalted at the right hand of God, as Messianic head of the new Israel.

Fourthly, the Holy Spirit in the church is the sign of Christ's present power and glory.

Fifthly, the Messianic Age will shortly reach its consummation in the return of Christ.

Finally, the *kērygma* always closes with an appeal for repentance, the offer of forgiveness and of the Holy Spirit, and the promise of "salvation," that is, of "the life of the Age to Come," to those who enter the elect community.[6]

From these two summaries, we can see that Dodd defined the good news primarily in terms of the postresurrection preaching of the apostles. The gospel, for Dodd, was fundamentally wrapped around the redemptive death, resurrection, ascension and glorification of Jesus of Nazareth as the Christ of God. For Paul and the early church, this was the gospel: "We proclaim Christ crucified, a stumbling block to Jews and foolishness to Gentiles, but to those who are the called, both Jews and Greeks, Christ the power of God and the wisdom of God" (1 Cor 1:23-24).

The church proclaimed the unequaled saving action of God in the life, ministry, death and resurrection of Jesus Christ. This message was *euangelion*. The good news in New Testament preaching was that God uniquely acted in and through Jesus Christ "reconciling the world to himself" (2 Cor 5:19). Thus the *euangelion*, or the *kērygma*, was the proclamation of God working through Christ and focusing on the quintessential salvific event of the crucifixion and resurrection of Jesus of Nazareth, the Christ.

A cursory reading of modern and contemporary materials written about evangelism shows that they ground their understanding almost exclusively on the postresurrection preaching of the apostles, whose perspective of good news was grounded on the crucified Christ, his resurrection and subsequent exaltation (Rom 1:4; 1 Cor 15:1-28.). Vernon Stanfield tacitly followed this approach when he suggested that evangelistic preaching declares "the mighty redemptive acts of God in Christ" and when he wrote that "evangelistic preaching is the proclamation of the good news concerning the redemptive acts of God in Christ."[7] Robert Menzies defined evangelistic preaching as proclamation of the "saving facts of the Gospel."[8] My interpretation is that what Stanfield meant by "redemptive acts" and what Menzies meant by "saving facts" is none other than the crucifixion, death and resurrection of Jesus Christ. But, as essential and necessary as that portion of the *euangelion* is, it does not complete the picture of the New Testament witness concerning the gospel.

So as not to be misunderstood, I assume that no evangelical Christian would argue about the salvific import of those events in the life of Jesus of Nazareth as a basis for Christian faith. However, my concern here is to ask whether solely emphasizing the events of the passion of Jesus Christ as the good news is theologically complete. Does the *euangelion* include more than a tacit mention of the life and ministry of Jesus and the preaching of his disciples? Is Jesus' own understanding of good news broader than the events of his death and resurrection?

Remember, we are attempting to learn exactly what *euangelion*—good news—is. Rather than confining our study to Paul's writings and apostolic preaching, the four Gospels themselves—often overlooked, except for the passion narratives, when it comes to defining evangelism—provide ample evidence to broaden an understanding of the good news. Don't forget, the early church referred to the Gospel writers as evangelists. This title alone hints at what the early church thought the *euangelion* included.

Mark's Gospel begins with the declaration "The beginning of the good news of Jesus Christ, the Son of God" (Mk 1:1). This statement implies that the entire ministry of Jesus of Nazareth is good news. Mark introduces the beginning of Jesus' Galilean ministry with the words "Jesus came to Galilee, proclaiming the good news of God, and saying, 'The time is fulfilled, and the kingdom of God has come near; repent, and believe in the good news' " (Mk 1:14-15). Matthew reports that "Jesus went throughout Galilee, teaching in their synagogues and proclaiming the good news of the kingdom and curing every disease and every sickness among the people" (Mt 4:23; see also 9:35). Luke recounts the angel's heralding Jesus' birth to the shepherds: "I am bringing you good news of great joy for all the people: to you is born this day in the city of David a Savior, who is the Messiah, the Lord" (Lk 2:10-11). Luke also records that John the Baptizer proclaimed good news to the people (Lk 3:18).

What gospel was Jesus proclaiming? What was the good news he called his hearers to believe? He certainly was not preaching about his crucifixion, death and resurrection at this point in his ministry; such preaching would not have made sense to his hearers. What did the angel mean by "good news" in his announcement to the shepherds? Certainly not that a child was born who would be crucified. That announcement would not have been good news to the shepherds; that message would have provoked fear, not dispelled it. The angel's concern was to put fear to rest—"Do not be afraid" (Lk 2:10). Messianic hope in first-century Judaism did not comprehend a crucified Messiah. So what was the angels' "good news of great joy" about the recently born Savior? What good news was John the Baptist preaching to the people? These events all took place long before the death and resurrection of Jesus, indicating that there must have been some *euangelion* that was a precursor to the postresurrection good news.

What about the preaching of the disciples in the Gospels? Mark records that Jesus appointed twelve to be with him and sent them out "to proclaim the message and to have authority to cast out demons" (Mk 3:14-15). Later in Mark's Gospel, Jesus called the Twelve to him and sent them in pairs on a preaching mission: "they went out and proclaimed that all should repent.

They cast out many demons, and anointed with oil many who were sick and cured them" (Mk 6:12-13). Matthew narrates the sending of the twelve disciples on their preaching task in the following way: "Go nowhere among the Gentiles, and enter no town of the Samaritans, but go rather to the lost sheep of the house of Israel. As you go, proclaim the good news, 'The kingdom of heaven has come near.' Cure the sick, raise the dead, cleanse the lepers, cast out demons" (Mt 10:5-8). Luke records the sending out of the Twelve this way: "Then Jesus called the twelve together and gave them power and authority over all demons and to cure diseases, and he sent them out to proclaim the kingdom of God and to heal" (Lk 9:1-2). Following Jesus' instructions, "they departed and went through the villages, bringing [preaching] the good news and curing diseases everywhere" (Lk 9:6). Only Luke records Jesus' sending a group of seventy whose mission was to cure the sick and to preach that "the kingdom of God has come near to you" (Lk 10:9).

What message did Jesus charge the disciples to proclaim? What was the aim of the preaching mission of the Twelve? Jesus charged them to preach a call to repentance. On what basis were they to repent? If we were to answer in light of our post-resurrection theology, we would say repentance was based on a faithful response to the self-giving love of Christ on the cross. But the cross was nowhere in the mind of those disciples. Therefore, on what did they ground their summons to repentance? Then, what did Jesus mean when he told them to preach the good news that the kingdom of heaven was near?

What about Jesus' preaching ministry? What did Jesus mean by good news? Matthew's Gospel says that Jesus inaugurated his Galilean ministry with the words "Repent, for the kingdom of heaven has come near" (Mt 4:17). As mentioned above, Mark reports that Jesus proclaimed "the good news of God, . . . saying, 'The time is fulfilled, and the kingdom of God has come near; repent, and believe in the good news' " (Mk 1:14-15). And later

Jesus said, " 'Let us go on to the neighboring towns, so that I may proclaim the message there also; for that is what I came out to do.' And he went throughout Galilee, proclaiming the message in their synagogues and casting out demons" (Mk 1:38-39).

Luke records the pivotal scene in Jesus' ministry that set the tone for Luke's entire Gospel:

When he came to Nazareth, where he had been brought up, he went to the synagogue on the sabbath day, as was his custom. He stood up to read, and the scroll of the prophet Isaiah was given to him. He unrolled the scroll and found the place where it was written:

"The Spirit of the Lord is upon me,
　　because he has anointed me
　　　　to bring good news to the poor.
He has sent me to proclaim release to the captives
　　and recovery of sight to the blind,
　　　　to let the oppressed go free,
　　to proclaim the year of the Lord's favor."

And he rolled up the scroll, gave it back to the attendant, and sat down. The eyes of all in the synagogue were fixed on him. Then he began to say to them, "Today this scripture has been fulfilled in your hearing." (Lk 4:16-21)

Does this introductory sermon point to Jesus' own understanding of the gospel he preached and charged his disciples to proclaim? I think so. Jesus views the very ministry to which he sees himself called as a fulfillment of Isaiah's prophetic summons. Jesus' ministry itself, as he understood it, was the genesis of God's *euangelion* to the world. "This was no ordinary good news and no ordinary messenger," wrote Michael Green. "It was nothing less than God's long-awaited salvation, proclaimed by the Messiah Himself. God had indeed come to the rescue of a world in need. No wonder, then, that it became known as *to euangelion,* the good news."[9]

I concur with Michael Green's idea that we should move away from truncated, impoverished and narrow definitions of evangelism. In our authentic concern to preach for conversion, we limit the very message of good news. Again, so as not to be misunderstood, I believe that conversion is paramount to evangelism. I agree with Will Willimon when he says, "Evangelism expects and promises transformation."[10] Conversion is not merely having people shift from one form of Christianity to another—not Baptists becoming Episcopalians or Presbyterians becoming Roman Catholics. Nor is it the dictionary definition of a change in which one adopts a new religion, faith or belief. Conversion is a radical transformation, the changing of the very nature and essence of who we are, brought about by God.

The good news is not only *about* grace; it *is* grace. The good news is not about what we do. The gospel is not news about which we have the luxury of giving our intellectual assent and making up our minds. I like Willimon's idea of the gospel being *intrusive news* that "evokes a new set of practices, a complex of habits, a way of living in the world, discipleship."[11] These ideas broaden our comprehension of preaching for conversion.

The contemporary evangelist's claim that "Jesus died for your sins. Accept what Christ did for you on the cross and have everlasting life" is unquestionably good news. But it's only part of the *euangelion*. Some evangelistic preaching makes salvation sound like a "respond-now, experience-later" proposition. The *euangelion* is likened to a financial transaction where a customer invests now for some future heavenly returns. A popular evangelistic approach is to ask a person a question such as "If you were to die today and God asked you, 'Why should I let you into heaven?' what would you say?" Notice the implication? Salvation is merely heaven-bound. The good news becomes totally ego-centered and self-serving. The motivation for responding to the gospel depreciates into a selfish loving of God for self's sake and not a grateful response to God's love and grace. We respond to the good news to keep our "hides from burning in hell," says the evangelist. Such evangelism plays into the modern fixation of getting something for nothing, while simultaneously saying that the good news has little import for today. It makes redemption a futuristic wish, echoed in singing "When we all get to heaven, what a day of rejoicing that will be!"

If the gospel is not an insurance policy for heaven, then what, exactly, is the good news? What is the basis of New Testament *kērygma*? What should we proclaim when we preach evangelistically? On what is evangelism based? If we look to Jesus' sermon in the synagogue at Nazareth, the answer to our questions begins to crystallize. The gospel is good news precisely because of its *nowness*. Jesus said, "The kingdom of heaven has come near." The good news is that God has invaded human history, inaugurating a reign that demands a new way of looking at life, today. The good news inaugurates a new worldview, a new order of thinking, a new way of making meaning, a new way of treating people, a new way of glimpsing who we are in the sight of God. Walter Brueggemann writes, "The gospel is the news that distorted patterns of power have been broken; the reception of the gospel is the embrace of radically transformed patterns of social relationships."[12]

Jesus said, "The Spirit of the Lord is upon me, because he has anointed me to bring good news to the poor." The good news is for the poor—those daily surrounded by bad news, those who wake up every day wondering why they have been forgotten, asking why God has deserted them, why their lives are so full of suffering. They are used to being reminded by some televangelist that if they were faithful—really believed—God would bless them. "Just place your hands on the TV and be healed. Just have faith and mail in your pledge. God wants you to prosper!" they are told.

But Jesus' good news is for all people, not only the poor who have been duped by popular religion and hucksters of free grace. Isn't that what the angel said? "I am bringing you good news of great joy for *all the people.*" At a time when the gap between the haves and the have-nots continues to spread, when people's worth is measured not by who they are but by what they own, Jesus' message breaks through like the first robin's song of spring. The good news for the poor is that they are not forgotten. The good news for all people is that Jesus remembers the forgotten masses—those who are forgotten by society and those who are forgotten by the church. Jesus began his sermon by first remembering them.

Jesus understood that he was being sent "to proclaim release to the captives and recovery of sight to the blind, to let the oppressed go free." The good news for Jesus is a freeing word. The gospel liberates; the good news emancipates. It calls for the release of those who are captive, for sight to those who are blind, and freedom for those who are oppressed. Jesus saw his ministry as a fulfillment of Isaiah's prophecy (Is 61:1-3; compare 35:1-6, 10). He was not spiritualizing these radical ideas, nor was he suggesting that the fulfillment of them was to be found merely in heaven. Jesus' good news is not a foggy vision of some future hope. It is not a romanticized idea of angels floating in heaven and evening strolls down streets of gold. Remember, his first remark after he closed the scroll was "Today this scripture has been fulfilled in your hearing." Not "in the sweet by and by" but *today.*

John the Baptist sent some of his followers to ask Jesus if he was the promised one or should they expect another. Remember Jesus' answer? "Go and tell John what you have seen and heard: the blind receive their sight, the lame walk, the lepers are cleansed, the deaf hear, the dead are raised, the poor have good news brought to them" (Lk 7:22; see also Mt 11:4-5). The good news breaks into the world with liberating power.

We no longer have to be held captive by our selfishness, by our culture's materialism, by the alienation we feel from our neighbors, by the loneliness we experience even when surrounded by people, by our sense of inadequacy to make any difference with our lives. The good news heralds a new way of facing life, a new way for naming our existence. The gospel opens our eyes to life that encompasses more than the accumulation of possessions—that relationships are precious, that people have innate worth because they have been created in God's image. They are not only hearers of the good news but participants in making its claims upon the world a reality.

God invades history to lay claim on creation and to participate in the process of re-creating it. The good news invites us to participate actively in that celebration. God is in the business of saving us from our own oppression, removing the shackles of our sin and setting us free. Isn't that what Jesus meant when he proclaimed the year of the Lord's favor? The joy and freedom and restoration associated with the year of jubilee (Lev 25:8-12) are here, now! What we have tried to do for ourselves—unsuccessfully—God has done for us in and through Jesus Christ. That's good news!

Of course, such news was scandalous to those who thought they had God fully understood. Religious leaders who spend their time talking about God and studying the Scriptures should know better. J. B. Philips reminded us that we cannot keep God in a box.[13] But religious leaders, of any age and any theological persuasion, often confuse their understanding of God for the true God. The religious establishment in Jesus' time could not tolerate blatant opposition to their authority. In fact, the word was quickly spreading that Jesus taught as one who had authority, not like the scribes. If you want to create a problem with the religious establishment, just get people to start calling into question their way of looking at things.

The good news that Jesus and his disciples preached not only didn't make sense to the leadership, it made them mad—so mad that they couldn't stand it any longer. They took matters into their own hands and, as a former professor used to say, "Drove God out of his world onto a tree!" They thought they could silence Jesus by killing him. Luke reminds us, however, that truth cannot be silenced. The stones themselves would cry out if someone, if anyone, tried to silence the truth (Lk 19:40).

On the first day of the week following the crucifixion, God raised Jesus Christ from the dead. The shackles of death could not hold him. The release he had proclaimed to the captives—the liberating gospel—was now manifested in his own resurrection. Jesus fulfilled the gospel he proclaimed. The good news that began with the proclamation of the angels at his birth is brought to completion. Yet the announcement of the angels at the tomb—"He is not here, but has risen" (Lk 24:5)—thunders the good news of Jesus Christ's breaking even the confines of time and space. "The proclamation of Easter news is not an end in itself. Its end is the generation of new life in the world."[14] The witness of the New Testament, especially that which is contained in the Gospels, sees the resurrection as the apex of Jesus' entire ministry—a reminder that not even a tomb can contain this good news. I agree with Brueggemann's assessment: "The news that God has triumphed means that a transformed life, i.e., one changed by the hearing of the news, works to bring more and more of life, personal and public, under the rule of this world-transforming, slave-liberating, covenant-making, promise-keeping, justice-commanding God."[15]

The apostle Paul's statement "For freedom Christ has set us free" (Gal 5:1) prompts us to claim our freedom *from* bondage *to* the potential for living life within God's kingdom and becoming active participants in making the kingdom of heaven available and real in the world. Or, as Paul wrote to the Colossians, "He has rescued us from the power of darkness and transferred us into the kingdom of his beloved Son, in whom we have redemption, the forgiveness of sins" (Col 1:13-14). C. H. Dodd put it this way: "The main burden of the *kērygma* is that the unprecedented has happened: God has visited and redeemed His people."[16] That news is *good* indeed!

A Theology for Evangelistic Preaching

Returning to C. H. Dodd's dichotomy of *kērygma* and *didachē*, I suggest that evangelistic preaching include both, because the New Testament *euangelion* includes both. Evangelistic preaching should be addressed to those who are foreigners to the province of God. It should make clear that the gospel—the *kērygma*—is an offer of faith. Invitation is at the heart of the gospel; the good news requests people's presence and participation. The message that God has acted in Jesus Christ for those outside the confines of God's reign represents the miracle of good news (Rom 5:8). However, much that is being written about evangelistic preaching presumes only a conversion motive; hence, the tacit understanding that the good news is *only* for the strangers in our midst. But the overwhelming truth saturating this good news does not complete its work when we become citizens; its work then begins in earnest.

The gospel denotes God's breaking into human history, redeeming people from their sins, and liberating them for life in God's realm. The catechetical preaching—*didachē*—designed to guide and instruct believers in the faith so as to uplift and strengthen their believing communities represents an intricate part of the gospel. Living within the province of God means learning how to be effective, faithful citizens; we thrive on both *kērygma* and *didachē*. The gospel makes foreigners into citizens and helps citizens remember the purpose of their citizenship. And lest we ever forget—even we who become the religious establishment—once we were foreigners to this gospel ourselves (1 Pet 2:10).

Richard Armstrong captures my interpretation of evangelistic preaching with his definition: "Evangelism is proclaiming in word and deed the good news of the kingdom of God, and calling people to repentance, to personal faith in Jesus Christ as Lord and Savior, to active membership in the church, and to obedient service in the world."[17]

In the broadest sense, one could say that all biblical preaching contains *euangelion,* because the Bible portrays a God who longs to have fellowship with us—such news is certainly good. Evangelistic preaching makes the revelation of this loving, intervening God real to hearers. For those outside the faith, the good news becomes an invitation to communal life within the fellowship of Christ. For those inside the faith, hearing and rehearing the gospel reminds us of our call to service within the church and in the world.

Evangelistic preaching embodies joy. After all, it is good news. Some evangelistic sermons I hear are full of gloom and doom. They remind people how inadequate they are, how sinful their actions are, how lustful their desires, how despicable their motives and how distasteful their lifestyles. Lectures, no matter their fidelity in diagnosing and naming the human condition, are heard with as much receptivity as a child has upon hearing for the umpteenth time that her room is a toxic waste dump. We can safely assume that most of the hearers of sermons, given that they have placed themselves within earshot of a sermon, already recognize the angst surrounding contemporary life. I have serious ethical problems with the evangelistic strategy of swinging them "low and slow over the fires of hell" before breaking the good news to them. Interestingly, Jesus never used that strategy.

People exhausted by the daily barrage of bad news can be told the consequences of sin without sensationalism and emotionalism. But we must inform them that the message of Jesus Christ is good news. The gospel coaxes those so accustomed to bad news to listen with new ears. Many may not know how to handle good news, especially such scandalous good news. We preachers can help by embodying the joy of the gospel. I'm not suggesting a sugarcoated, drippy joy of sentimentalism or romanticism. The gospel is unequaled, unmitigated joy—a blessedness that defies definition. Evangelistic preaching embodies such joy.

Evangelistic preaching acknowledges the scandalous nature of the good news. Lest we forget, though the gospel is good news, it is not cheap news, nor is it demand-free.

A person once came to Jesus and asked what he had to do to have eternal life. Jesus told him that if he wished to enter into eternal life, he must keep the commandments. He asked, "Which ones?" Jesus recited part of the Decalogue. "The young man said to him, 'I have kept all these; what do I still lack?' Jesus said to him, 'If you wish to be perfect, go, sell your possessions, and give the money to the poor, and you will have treasure in heaven; then come, follow me' " (Mt 19:16-22). We are hucksters of cheap grace if we peddle a gospel bereft of demands.

No doubt, the clarion call of the Reformation was justification by grace through faith: "For by grace you have been saved through faith, and this is not your own doing; it is the gift of God—not the results of works, so that no one may boast" (Eph 2:8-9). But the gospel is not only about becoming "saved"; it's also about living the "saved" life, or what theologians call sanctification. I am thoroughly convinced that the gospel includes both justification and sanctification. Our evangelistic preaching must not neglect either.

Remember, this good news, no matter how effectively communicated, may not gain a hearing. Will Willimon reminds us that the gospel is an intrusive word. It cuts against the grain of societal wisdom. It calls into question rational sensibilities. It sticks its finger in the face of rabid relativism. It demands more than intellectual assent. It does not tolerate dilution in the company of modernism, postmodernism or postpostmodernism.

Our task in evangelistic preaching is not to adapt the gospel to contemporary culture so that people will respond to it. Our goal remains to communicate the gospel clearly so that they do not confuse it with their own desires, wishes or religious longings. In so doing, their decision to respond to, turn away from or further probe the gospel is based on their unclouded hearing of it.

Evangelistic preaching has no need to apologize for discussing subjects such as repentance and conversion. Our investigation of the New Testament showed that repentance and conversion arise from the heart of the *euangelion*. Evangelistic preaching surpasses the dissemination of moralisms, believed by certain preachers to be the cure for the downfall of modern society. Preaching to gain assent for particular moral behaviors undermines the conversional nature of the gospel. The gospel implies much more than doing nice things for people or being an upright and moral person. What would be uniquely Christian about such behavior?

Many upright, moral people remain outside the Christian faith. Even some evangelicals confuse moral values for converted faith. The gospel invites a transformed life wrought by the action of a loving God (2 Cor 5:17). Such conversion is not merely behavior modification; a good psychologist could entice exemplary actions. Evangelistic preaching takes seriously the need for persons willingly to seek forgiveness of sin, to turn away from self-centeredness, to turn toward God, to submit themselves to the lordship of Christ, and to become faithful citizens of God's realm. Hence, the plea to repent and believe marked Jesus' preaching. Preaching evangelistically understands the depth of the sinful human condition and the need for God's intervention.

Evangelistic preaching holds a delicate tautness between the present and future tense of God's reign. Such tension manifests itself throughout the New Testament. We, as evangelists, often unwittingly, err on the side of pointing to the *futureness*—the eschatological side—of the gospel. Jesus' sermon in Nazareth clearly showed the gospel's immediacy: "Today this scripture has been fulfilled in your hearing." We should preach so that people recognize that the good news means *now* news. The converted life of which we spoke begins here and now.

Tom Long says that we begin now to learn and practice the language and customs of God's kingdom.[18] He equates the church with the language school for the kingdom. We begin now to treat people the way we will treat them in the kingdom. We begin now to love people the way we will love them in the kingdom. We begin now to love ourselves the way we will be loved in the kingdom. We begin now to do justice the way justice will be experienced in the kingdom. "What does the Lord require of you but to do justice, and to love kindness, and to walk humbly with your God?" asked the prophet Micah (Mic 6:8). When should this take place? Jesus says, "Today!" That the kingdom of God has come near seems remarkably good news.

Evangelistic preaching holds in balance the spiritual and the physical dimensions of our existence. In the Gospels, the good news preached by Jesus and the disciples was accompanied by healing, curing of disease, casting out demons and cleansing of lepers. The Gospels are replete with accounts of Jesus' tending to the physical and spiritual needs of people. The good news remains a holistic message. I once heard a preacher say, "Hungry bellies have no ears." He was commenting on this aspect of evangelistic preaching. Preaching the *euangelion* means bringing good news to feed their souls, but if their stomachs lack food, the gospel also requires sharing a meal (Jas 2:15-16). It may mean rolling up our sleeves and getting our hands dirty. It may mean emptying our pockets to care for somebody else's children. The good news speaks to body, soul, mind and spirit. Our evangelistic preaching can reflect no less.

Finally, evangelistic preaching emphasizes the liberating

character of the gospel. Some remain shackled by cancerous sin. Some suffer the bondage of unresolved grief. Some are physically imprisoned. Some experience the prison of abuse—sexual, physical and mental. Loneliness and self-doubt hold some people captive. Others endure captivity at the hands of the unrelenting demands of cultural success. Others are oppressed by the persistent hunt for their own solutions to the deepest dilemmas of life. *Release* remains the conspicuous feature of the gospel. Yet sometimes this aspect of the gospel becomes the most difficult to hear because its prospect for changing the future looms frightening.

Jesus' question to the man at the pool of Beth-zatha highlights the issue: "Do you want to be made well?" (Jn 5:6). At first glance the answer seems obvious. Of course he wants to be healed. Why else would he be here at a pool known for healing? But the discomfort of known pain may appear less threatening than the comfort of an unknown cure. Fear of repercussion for seeking release may prevent someone from stepping toward liberation. In a culture that prides itself on individualism and flaunts those who have pulled themselves up by their own strength, even the reliance on God appears as weakness. In a society that already feels liberated, good news of liberation seems naive at best. Perhaps freedom from pseudoliberation is the best word of all.

Summing Up

Think about the people you see every week: those you bump into in the grocery store; your accountant; your lawyer; your doctor; youth who hang out at the mall; a young urban professional who passes you on the expressway at breakneck speed in his BMW; a teenage, unmarried couple who discover that they are expecting a child; an alcoholic who swears never to "fall off the wagon" again; the out-of-control parent of a teenager; the child of an Alzheimer's patient; people ad infinitum—

people who need good news. The gospel of Jesus Christ is risky business because it liberates, it transforms, it offers us freedom, it demands faith. Most of the time we proclaim this good news when we ourselves don't fully comprehend the risks.

Evangelistic preaching helps make this incredible, unnerving, liberating gospel of Jesus Christ known to all who will hear, offering them a chance to respond. It really is good news. Now who's afraid of the big bad wolf?

3/It Sure Doesn't Look Like an Evangelistic Sermon

*O*ne problem with evangelistic sermons is that they look and sound like evangelistic sermons. When I reflect on some evangelistic services I've attended, I have discerned an implicit pattern, not only in the service itself but in the sermons. Revival services included certain hymns as standard-bearers, such as "Revive Us Again," "Send a Great Revival," "Pentecostal Power," "There Is Power in the Blood" and "The Old Rugged Cross." The sermons also had a particular tone, timbre and texture. I'm not talking about delivery style or the personality of the evangelist; I'm focusing on the sermon.

The evangelist often began with a humorous story or two, perhaps even a couple of jokes, presumably to make some connection with the congregation—to break the ice, so to speak. Then he described the topic at hand, often telling how the subject would be outlined: "This evening, we're going to look at five consequences of rejecting Christ." Then, the evangelist delineated the subject, point by point, often moving from biblical exposition, to explanation, to illustration, and to application for each of the sermon's major headings. The sermons developed logically and rationally, appealing to the reason and emotions of the congregation.

Movement through each of the main points was deductive and propositional. In other words, the position being maintained or put forward was stated first, with the presumption (by the preacher) that it was an indisputable, undeniable claim: for instance, "God wants *everyone* to be happy." The sermon's reasoning then moved deductively from this general claim to show its truth in specific situations: "God wants *you* to be happy." In deductive logic, the conclusion is drawn from the overriding premise. In this example the logic goes this way:

1. Major premise: God wants everyone to be happy.
2. Minor premise: You are one of "everyone."
3. Conclusion: Therefore God wants you to be happy.

After the evangelists unfolded each major point this way, the sermons typically climaxed with an emotional appeal. Again, the logic went, based on the propositions presented you can either reasonably accept or unreasonably reject what you've heard. In the services I'm describing, the evangelist offered an altar call or invitation for the congregation to respond to the message.

In general, then, the sermons looked like this:

I. Introduction
II. Body
    A. Main point
        1. Support (exposition, explanation, illustration)
        2. Support
    B. Main point
    C. Main point
    D. Main point
III. Conclusion
IV. Invitation

To find some concrete examples of this method, I went to the library at Southern Baptist Theological Seminary, where I teach preaching, and browsed the subject card catalog under the top-ic "Evangelistic Sermons." I randomly selected seven books of evangelistic sermons. Not exactly a scientific approach I con-fess, but I was just looking for examples.[1]

C. E. Autrey preached a sermon titled "Can We Believe in God?" I have outlined the sermon below, taking obvious cues from the manuscript.[2]

I. [Introduction] We shall try to answer the following ques-tions in this message: (1) Is God a reality? (2) What is He like? and (3) How may we know Him?

II. [Body]

A. Is There a Living God?

1. We believe that God is because the Bible says so.

2. We believe there is a God from the argument of *cause and effect.*

3. It is the common experience of people that God is real.

B. What Is God Like?

1. God is not a question mark in the sky at which we hurl prayers.

2. God is a person.

3. God is a Father of love.

4. Jehovah is a God of judgment.

C. How May We Know God?

1. We know God by reading the Bible.

2. We know God by association with God's people.

3. We know God by experience with Christ.

III. [Conclusion] A personal story about the day he authen-tically experienced God, ending with the words "I knew God was real for He had come into my soul. There was an abiding witness within me, that I was saved."

Another example is entitled "Religion or Christ," preached by Alan Walker.[3]

I. [Introduction] Walker describes a visit he made to the

United Nations, particularly to a small chapel near the entrance door. The smallness of the chapel in light of the complexity of world problems forced him to ask if the chapel and what it contained could help people find God. He answered by asserting that only Jesus Christ can help people find God. The introduction ends with the question "Why is Jesus Christ necessary?"

II. [Body: After each point, Walker gave two to three illustrations to demonstrate the truth of the statement]

    A. The Way to the Christian God: "First of all I suggest that Jesus Christ is absolutely essential because only through Him can we come to the Christian God."

    B. The Way into the Christian Church: "Secondly, I suggest that Jesus Christ is so essential to our life because He gives us the community of Christians called the Church."

    C. The Way to the Christian Conscience: "Again, I suggest that Jesus Christ is so essential because all of us need the conscience of Christ."

    D. The Way to Christian Salvation: "There is one other declaration that must be made. More than a chapel with silence, roses on a table, and curtained walls, Jesus Christ is absolutely essential because every one needs Him as Saviour."

III. [Conclusion] "Why is Jesus Christ necessary? He is necessary because the Saviour is necessary. We need not merely a chapel, with silence, curtained walls, and roses on a table. We need a lonely hill with the Cross on its rim, an empty tomb in a garden, and the Risen Christ, Saviour and Lord."

IV. [Invitation] "This is the need of all our hearts. Have you received Him? I offer you Christ."

Notice how both sermons generally follow the introductory example outline.

To return to discussing the sermons I heard preached, one strength of these sermons is their simplicity. Few would have trouble figuring out the evangelists' point. Not everyone would agree with the preachers' conclusions, but all would know where they stood. Another strength is the sermons' sense of urgency. They clearly come across as a matter of life and death. Of course, as in all preaching, some evangelists show more imagination than others, so some sermons are more interesting than others.

Some sermons weigh too heavily on the side of doctrinal exposition, dreadfully neglecting the life situations of the listening congregations. Other sermons rely so strongly on emotionalism that they are like cotton candy—they initially gratify the appetite, but the satisfaction is short-lived. Still, there is little doubt that they are evangelistic sermons. They look like evangelistic sermons. They sound like evangelistic sermons. They have that evangelistic-sermon texture and feel. Their design, structure and approach matches everyone's expectations. That's the very reason I have a problem with them, at least in terms of contemporary evangelistic preaching.

The sermons are grounded in some unspoken assumptions. One assumption is that once people know what is right, they will do what is right. The logic goes this way: the reason people do not respond to the gospel is that they are ignorant of the gospel. In the examples described, the goal of evangelistic sermons is to enlighten people's minds and remove their ignorance. I'm not sure that assumption ever contained validity, but it seems an especially naive understanding of human motivation today. Even James wrote that the demons recognize that there is only one God (Jas 2:19). It causes them to shudder, but they remain demons. James suggests that mere knowledge is not enough to prompt a change in attitude or behavior. Knowing what is right does not guarantee that people will act on that knowledge. Nevertheless, this presumption has directed sermon design.

The logic continues thus: if people act on the truth once they know it, we need only lay out the truth in a logical and straightforward way. So evangelists have designed sermons propositionally and deductively. Evangelistic sermons have been concerned with the communication of information—doctrinal, theological, biblical—believing that transformation occurs because of *right knowledge.*

Another premise under which many evangelistic sermons have been designed is that preachers are respected authorities on matters of religion, morals, values and life. Therefore, their interpretations of these subjects were correct and, to an extent, indisputable. Notice the way this presupposition has controlled how evangelistic sermons look. If the evangelist is a respected authority, then people take what the evangelist says at face value. The hearers might not like it, may not be happy with it or might have trouble agreeing with it, but who is going to question a *respected authority?* The evangelist must be right. Sermons merely have to communicate the evangelist's interpretation as clearly and straightforwardly as possible. Breaking the subject down into well-argued points, with some illustration and application, becomes the presumptive most effective and efficient way to present the truth claims of the gospel.

Moving from the sublime to the ridiculous, the logic became that evangelistic sermons *must* follow this pattern or plan. It became common practice for preachers to design evangelistic sermons that all looked pretty much alike. If you doubt my analysis, go to your local Christian book store and browse the sermon books. Find those under the title of evangelistic or revival sermons. A common title might be something like *100 Evangelistic Sermon Outlines.* Notice how similar the outline shapes are to the one I have been discussing. We preachers have succumbed to the fallacy that for a sermon to be evangelistic it must *look like* an evangelistic sermon.

The Form-Versus-Content Dilemma

Does an evangelistic sermon have to look like an evangelistic sermon to be evangelistic? Does sermon *form* or *content* determine if a sermon is evangelistic? At a first glance the answer appears obvious. But this question can be tricky to answer. Even in light of our above discussion, we must admit that there is no such thing as formless content. All content—the groceries we bring home from the store, the words to a favorite song, a passage of Scripture or a sermon—comes in some package. The question confronting us here is, How crucial is the relationship between form and content? In other words, What impact does the form have on that which it carries?

When it comes to groceries, packaging greatly affects contents. An insulated bag keeps a gallon of ice cream from melting. A plastic jug keeps milk from spilling. A Styrofoam container keeps a dozen eggs from being scrambled. Notice, however, that in these physical examples the package does not change the basic nature of what it contains. A square ice-cream container or a round ice-cream container changes the shape of the ice cream, but the ice cream itself remains unchanged. Its essence—the ingredients that make it ice cream—remains the same.

But when it comes to language, the matter becomes more tangled. Assume that the following words are lyrics from a song: "The dawning sun broke the night's bondage / reminds me of your endless love." The words, even as they stand, can have an impact on us. However, if the song is a ballad, we will understand the words in a certain way. If the song is rock and roll, the impact of the words changes. If the very same words are the text of a hymn, the effect on us is, again, totally different. With language, the way content is understood often lies in the influence of form. The form participates in making the content mean what it does.

Tom Long deals with the form-versus-content dilemma by

talking about "the form of the content."[4] He understands that the effect of language is not merely in the message (the content) but in the interrelationship between the message and its form. I think the reason for this interplay has to do with expectations. When a ballad begins to play, we recognize it as a ballad. We know from our experience of hearing other ballads what to expect when someone plays a ballad. We know that ballads are romantic songs telling a story, often containing a recurring refrain. That doesn't mean every ballad has to look and sound like every other ballad. If such were the case, the music would be boring. But the overall ballad form carries the verbal message in a particular way. We know this because we've heard ballads before.

When we sing in church, we sing hymns of faith. Hymns, by definition, are songs of praise and joy, or thanksgiving, to God. It's not just the words of hymns that let us know this. It's the nature of expectation of the hymn form itself. The genre sets forth certain expectations that the hymn will meet when we hear it sung. The function of the form in these cases is based on the expectations established as the form is presented to us.

The typical genre (form) for preaching is the sermon. When we hear the word *sermon* certain expectations come to mind. We assume some form of religious speech delivered as part of a church service. Like other discourse genres, the general form of a sermon meets the expectations of a listening congregation. That fact does not mean that every sermon must look or sound alike. Such similarity would be deadly for preaching. If the sermons we preach merely met the expectations of our hearers, the prophetic voice of preaching would be lost to the wind. If a sermon looks like an evangelistic sermon, and the people are anxiously awaiting an evangelistic sermon, then you're on safe ground. But, if the hearers are hostile to evangelism and the very form of the sermon says "evangelistic," bells and whistles sound. You're sunk before you set sail.

I am urging that we define preaching by its content and not by its form. We want to be cognizant that every sermon we preach will have some particular form, and that the form impacts the content. But the form does not define what kind of sermon it is; that is the province of the message preached. The gospel can be communicated in a variety of ways. The four evangelists who wrote the Gospels preached the good news differently than Paul. According to Luke, Paul packaged the good news differently when he spoke to Gentiles than he did when he preached in synagogues. The message didn't change, but the way of communicating the message was adapted to its context.

Can Inductive Sermons Be Evangelistic?

Students have asked me if inductive sermons can be evangelistic. It's a good question. Whereas much has been written about inductive preaching, it's probably good for me to give my understanding, at least, of the inductive enterprise.[5] I will begin by explaining more fully the deductive approach as a basis for comparison. Earlier I said that in deductive logic the conclusion arises from the overriding premise. We have examples of deductive logic in the following forms known as syllogisms:

☐ Major premise: All people are mortal.

   Minor premise: Socrates is a person.

   (Therefore) Conclusion: Socrates is mortal.

☐ Major premise: All green apples are sour.

   Minor premise: This is a green apple.

   (Therefore) Conclusion: This apple is sour.

☐ Major premise: Hot ovens will burn your hand if you touch them.

   Minor premise: This is a hot oven.

   (Therefore) Conclusion: If you touch this oven, you will burn your hand.

These examples follow one form of deductive reasoning. The

logic moves from the general principle (*all* people are mortal) to the specific situation (Socrates is mortal). In a sermon based on Mark 5, Clovis G. Chappell said, "Now, what did Jesus do for this demoniac? He gave him a unified personality. That he can do for you and me."[6] The outline of the sermon before this statement argued for Jesus' ability to unify troubled personalities. He did this for the demoniac *then;* therefore he can do it for you *now.* The logic moves from the general principle to the specific situation—first from the demoniac, then to us. At the heart of this logical approach lies *an unquestioned acceptance of the proposition that makes up the major premise.*

Preaching based on this deductive approach continues to be prevalent among evangelical ministers. Beginning with a clearly stated thesis (major premise), the sermon develops by showing how the general truth claims are appropriated in the listener's situation. As we have already seen, it is one way of forming sermons.

What happens, though, if a congregation does not accept the major premise? In deductive logic, if the major premise appears unacceptable, there's no place for the logic to move. In the third example above, what if someone said, "I don't believe hot ovens will burn your hand if you touch one"? You could move to the minor premise, pointing out that the oven before you is a hot oven. But the conclusion cannot be drawn, deductively, that the person will burn her hand. She disagrees with your deduction because she gives no credence to your point of origin. In other words, the proposition is groundless as far as she is concerned. To prove your point, you could suggest she touch the hot oven. But once you move from your major premise to seeking to prove your point through experience, you have shifted to a new ball game. Now you're on the playing field of *inductive* logic.

Induction derives general principles from particular instances. Inductive logic moves from particular experience to forming a general principle. Most of the life-experience wisdom we have, we have learned inductively. You can tell a child until your face turns blue that he shouldn't come near a hot oven or she will get burned. Most kids learn the truth of that proposition when they touch a hot oven. What they failed to learn deductively, they discovered inductively. Chances are they will avoid hot ovens in the future—at least for a while.

Here is an example of inductive logic: Suppose you have never eaten a green apple, and no one has told you what to expect when you eat green apples. You bite into one and discover that it tastes sour. Can you draw a conclusion about all green apples based on your experience with one? Not yet. But after you've eaten a half dozen or so green apples, though no one has said anything to you about them, you draw the conclusion that green apples are sour. That is the general principle you discovered inductively through experience. The conclusion you've drawn is "Green apples are sour."

That conclusion will hold until you taste a green apple that is not sour, and then the conclusion will shift only mildly to "*Most* green apples are sour." Notice that inductive logic does not have the weakness that one must begin with agreement to a proposition so as to reach the conclusion. The conclusion is drawn through an informal process of discovery.

Most evangelists structure evangelistic sermons following the deductive model. The preacher states a proposition at the beginning of the sermon and sets out to prove its veracity and to apply its truth: for example, "Jesus Christ is the same yesterday, today and forever." This method has been taught in evangelical seminaries for years and has been used successfully by evangelists and pastors alike. To presume that this model represents the only way to preach evangelistic sermons, however, is to fall prey to the deception of defining preaching by its form and not by its content.

Don't discard the effective approaches you now use. Add to

them. Every major preaching book written in the last century has called for variety in all types of preaching. That advice holds no less true for evangelistic preaching.

In some ways the inductive approach may actually be the better approach for evangelistic sermons because it inherently overcomes the problem of negative listener bias. If the hearers do not agree with the propositions set forth in the deductive model, or if they are resistant or downright hostile toward the subject, the deductive approach creates more problems than it can ever justifiably answer. Pastoral preaching seems more easily suited to the deductive model. With pastoral preaching, we typically preach to inform, to encourage, to inspire, to provide counsel, to speak on behalf of our listeners or to affirm the congregation. It's likely in such circumstances that your hearers would be more open to a sermon that moved from a stated thesis to applied conclusions, since they already feel some harmony or agreement with the thesis. Evangelistic preaching presumes that though the message is good news, there may still be resistance to it. In such cases taking an inductive approach makes better sense.

Biblical models of the inductive strategy abound. Nathan led David to a conclusion rather than presenting a thesis and arguing for its truth and acceptance (2 Sam 12). How much of the message do you think David would have heard if Nathan had begun with a proposition? "David, your unwillingness to confront your sin makes you unacceptable in God's eyes." That statement rings true, but caught so red-handedly, the king could have rationalized away his behavior. Nathan's inductive approach, with the ewe lamb story, disarmed the resistance, confronted David authentically with his sin and led to repentance and restoration.

Amos indicted Israel's enemies in a series of parallel allegations before pronouncing God's judgment on Israel itself (Amos 1:3—2:16). This inductive movement kept resistance from building. When Amos finally accused the Israelites of similar transgressions, they could do little but fall under appropriate judgment. Amos drew the Israelites to conclusions through their own discovery and discernment of the veracity of his message.

Although the apostle Paul often preached and communicated deductively, the sermon at the Areopagus appears inductive in tone (Acts 17:22-31). Even with this strategy, the text says, some scoffed at what they heard about the resurrection of the dead. If Paul had begun the sermon by speaking of the resurrection, their resistance to that truth might have been too much for any of them to overcome. As it was, Luke notes, some said, "We will hear you again about this," and still others joined Paul and became believers (Acts 17:32-34). Sounds to me like good biblical evidence that some were persuaded to believe because Paul used an inductive approach.

Some critics of inductive preaching have labeled it everything from a theological Rorschach test to a groundless concern for experience devoid of any legitimate truth claims. (It sounds as though it's being labeled *relativism*.) Some might argue that all truth cannot be learned through experience. Perhaps they have a point. *All* truth may not be teachable through experience. But one could argue that *all* truth cannot be expressed in propositions either.

The Christian faith is rooted in the mystery of revelation. In the Bible, revelation is mediated more through human experience than it is through propositional discourse. I am not arguing for one model exclusively. I am suggesting that induction is an orphan when it comes to evangelistic preaching. That's a shame, because I feel it is a model well suited for evangelism.

Like any method, inductive preaching is prone to abuse by its users. No method solely claims the high ground for presenting sermons. That's the very point I have been trying to make. Sermons are defined by content and not by form. The inductive approach is one, and only one, model for sermon design. I argue for it strongly here because it is the neglected model in evangelistic preaching. And yet its very form lends itself to evangelistic content.

In actual preaching, our methods may, as Ralph Lewis intimates, be hybrid. That is, our sermons are probably either deductive-inductive or inductive-deductive (the former term indicating the predominant model used). As a kind of learning exercise, try evaluating some sermons you've preached over the past year or two. Based on the descriptions of deduction and induction provided here, see how many sermons fall under one heading or the other. The sample sermons contained in chapter six basically follow the inductive or the inductive-deductive model, giving further evidence that inductive sermons can clearly communicate the *euangelion*.

In summation, what typifies the major difference between deductive and inductive sermons? Deductive sermons begin with propositions to be explained or proven and then applied to life experience. Inductive sermons lead hearers to the truth of the gospel by showing its relationship to their life experience and by helping them discover that this relevance is founded in the gospel.

What about other sermon forms, such as narrative sermons or monologue sermons using biblical characters? Can these forms be used for evangelistic preaching? My colleagues Raymond Bailey and James Blevins often preach monologue sermons in full biblical costume. They've written a wonderful book on the subject, laying out the theological and practical aspects of this sermon form.[7] The sermons in their book, as well as their own preaching of monologue sermons, attest that monologue sermons can certainly communicate the *euangelion*.

It ought to be clear by now that we should define sermons by content and not by form. The particular form of the sermon should be based on the biblical message and the desired outcome you hope to achieve for the sermon. Certain forms lend themselves more effectively to certain preaching goals than do others. The decision to choose an inductive model over a deductive one (or vice versa) is based more on the strategy of the particular sermon than on whether it is an evangelistic or pastoral sermon. Either type of sermon could use either logical form of composition.

A dramatic monologue sermon based on the apostle Paul or Mary Magdalene could certainly be evangelistic. The content of the sermon, the purpose you have in mind for the sermon and whether the sermon communicates the good news determines if it is evangelistic. The monologue *form* is subservient to the sermon's evangelistic purpose. Obviously, the selection of the monologue form will set up certain hearer expectations, but they may not expect to hear an evangelistic sermon. That may be your best ally for having them experience the good news for the first time or all over again in a fresh, new way.

Characteristics of Evangelistic Sermons

So what does an evangelistic sermon look like if it is defined by content and not by form? The substance of evangelistic sermons is the *euangelion* I outlined in chapter two. *Evangelistic sermons clearly proclaim God's good news.* They make intelligible the unique action of God in Jesus Christ to redeem and reconcile the world to himself. The pinnacle of this reconciling message appears in the atoning death and triumphal resurrection of Jesus Christ. This reality, when rightly fathomed, coaxes us to explore the rest of the gospel landscape. The good news encompasses not just the death and resurrection of Jesus Christ but the full significance of God's becoming flesh and dwelling among us.

God has always been an actor in human history. The creation of human history itself was the result of God's acting. The uniqueness of the incarnation signals God's personal intervention into that history. The world and all its inhabitants can no longer be the same after God walked in history. Our relationships, how we make sense out of life, how we cope with anxiety, the way we respond in grief, the way we approach the forgotten people we pass on the street, our actions on behalf of ignored, lonely people are significantly transformed because of God's loving activity in Christ. Sermons that *intentionally* announce this breaking of God into human history are evangelistic.

By communicating the good news intelligibly, I don't mean conforming the gospel to the perceived needs of contemporary hearers. The gospel doesn't need modernization. Though it began more than two thousand years ago, the gospel remains marked by immediacy. It is good news *now!* By its very nature it already speaks to the contemporary needs of people, because the gospel roots itself in the joys and dilemmas of human life. Difficult to hear for some, unbelievable for others, but a timeless message of justice, grace and love just the same. Evangelistic sermons herald this already-present reality of God's love, care and sovereign reign.

In practice this requires preachers to compose sermons that maintain the timelessness of the gospel while communicating it in ways that contemporary hearers can comprehend in their life situations. People are interested in hearing about people. Enliven evangelistic sermons with stories of how the gospel touched and transformed the lives of real people, people you know. Can't think of any, you say? Maybe the gospel is not as life transforming as preachers claim. If you can't think of examples or stories, chances are the idea you're working with is not clear enough yet. Work on it more until you can *see* that about which you are talking.

Fred Craddock urges preachers to turn ideas into people. His advice captures my concern. You know the adage "A picture is worth a thousand words." Provide a verbal picture of someone whose life is different because they encountered Christ, and you won't have to waste "a thousand words" defending the gospel's truth. Don't just *tell* it; *show* your hearers what the world can look like if they take the gospel seriously. Through rich images, contemporary stories and examples, and the testimony of someone whose life was changed, you can show the timeless character of the gospel in your sermons. Showing rather than telling is an axiom of good fiction writing, but it is also a sound means of conveying truth in evangelistic preaching.

Evangelistic sermons should not make the gospel sound cheap or demandless. We have already shown that at the heart of evangelism is God's action on behalf of humanity. The Bible makes clear that the initiating movement is from God toward us. Notice I said "the initiating movement." God's action does require human reaction. Passive reception is clearly not what Jesus or the disciples expected. The Gospels are replete with examples of radical actions taken as a response to the good news. Just ask Zacchaeus!

Sermons that preach easy grace are not evangelistic. We could effortlessly succumb to preaching what people want to hear. Such speech always musters a crowd and elicits praise and accolades. The point remains that the gospel really isn't what people want to hear. It doesn't tell them how to make loads of money ("If you wish to be perfect, go, sell your possessions, and give the money to the poor, and you will have treasure in heaven; then come, follow me"—Mt 19:21). It doesn't tell them to be all they can be, no matter the cost to others ("Those who find their life will lose it, and those who lose their life for my sake will find it"—Mt 10:39). It offers no comfortable lifestyle ("If any want to become my followers, let them deny themselves and take up their cross and follow me"—Mt 16:24). It requires a different life ethic, an altered view of life ("Let anyone among you who is without sin be the first to throw a stone at her"—Jn 8:7). No, this is not demand-free, "no obligation, completely satisfied or your money back" news. This is the gospel of Jesus

Christ. Evangelistic sermons must hold in tension the gospel's grace and demands when proclaiming Jesus' good news.

Evangelistic sermons are not angry harangues about people's laziness or sinfulness. They are not sermons about "mini skirts, revenge, burglary, rock music" or other pet "social ills" an evangelist happens to be railing against that week. Evangelistic sermons confront people with the God of creation and offer them the possibility to be loved, forgiven, redeemed and commissioned for service.

Evangelistic sermons avoid the jargons and clichés of organized religion without neglecting the richness of a theological vocabulary. Sermons replete with religious sound bites, popular coded religious phrases and trite God-talk make no sense to those outside the faith. Why use them if one intention of evangelistic sermons is to speak to those persons?

Yet people do need a language that enables them to express and understand the transcendent mysteries of life. In a lecture Tom Long urged preachers to provide people with a theological vocabulary—that is, the ability to talk authentically about the mysteries of life using words such as *faith, hope, love, sin, forgiveness, reconciliation* and *redemption*. Long argues that people have lost their theological vocabulary and therefore have no way to talk about mystery or transcendence in their lives. An evangelistic sermon should provide a language of faith to all who hear. But it should be mindful that some uninitiated may need help understanding even the most basic terms of the faith.

Evangelistic sermons offer acceptance to those who are not a part of the ekklēsia. For those who feel forgotten, neglected and shunned, evangelistic sermons herald God's acceptance and remembrance. For curious seekers, evangelistic sermons unpretentiously unfold God's offer of kingdom life. For those who think and feel that they don't need God or don't want to be a part of the church, evangelistic sermons provide a nonthreatening invitation to "hear you again about this" (Acts 17:32). But evangelistic sermons are not afraid of seeking conversion. Because the gospel is not just good news but is life-encountering, life-transforming news, conversion abides at its heart.

Evangelistic sermons need not neglect the authentic traditions of the faith. If there are strangers in your midst, remember that they have come to you. They should expect some words they hear to be somewhat strange, some customs they see practiced to be somewhat foreign. When they come to church, they really have arrived in a new and different world. They have entered, could we dare say, something like the kingdom of God. Like a traveler visiting Europe or Asia, they come expecting something different from what they are used to week in and week out. Perhaps hope of an escape from their mundane existence has brought them as seekers. Rather than throwing out our traditions to appease our visitors, why not let them in on the richness of our customs? After all, we want them to get a feel for what it is like to be God's people. Perhaps if they learn to see the value of what we say and do, and learn to enjoy the customs we practice, they will want to be a part of our community.

This advice flies in the face of some conventional wisdom of church growth. Certain church-growth experts believe and urge that what people need and what they are looking for when they come to church is the familiar—familiar music, familiar media forms, familiar surroundings, familiar sights, sounds and smells, familiar movements, familiar speech. These advocates of the church-growth movement have a "familiar fetish." They advocate creating worship services that look, sound, smell and taste like what seekers are seeking. How do they know what seekers are seeking? *They* ask *them* what they are looking for in church.

Sounds like a great way to do theology to me: "You're not seeking to take up your cross this week? Well, then, how can we make you comfortable with the gospel?" Evangelistic sermons that perpetuate a cultural mindset offer no good news at all. We can welcome seekers in our midst by helping them see

God. The authentic traditions and worship patterns of our faith do not need to be discarded for this to happen.

Contrary to popular notions, *evangelistic sermons are not just for the strangers in our midst.* These sermons also remind believers of the good news. They remind them of their citizenship. They help them remember who they are and to what they have been called and commissioned. As royal priests, we are partners with God in helping people recognize their chosenness in Jesus Christ. Evangelistic sermons rekindle the gospel mandate within believers. The gospel is meaning-making. It helps make sense out of life for strangers and citizens of God's kingdom alike.

Evangelistic sermons are liberating sermons. They make clear the clarion call to freedom trumpeted through the gospel. By their tone, their language, the stories they use, the form they take, evangelistic sermons offer liberation. When rightly understood, the gospel of Jesus Christ frees us *from* ourselves *to* God.

Evangelistic sermons should have an invitational tone. This idea models the gospel itself; the gospel is invitational. Evangelistic sermons should offer people some type of opportunity to respond to what they have heard. We will speak more about this subject specifically in chapter seven. It is enough to say here that evangelistic sermons look invitational. By their design and tone, they are an offer to experience kingdom life with kingdom people.

Summing Up

Now that I have defined good news, presented a theology for evangelistic preaching and offered a new look at evangelistic sermons, our attention moves to the Bible as the source for evangelistic sermons. The next two chapters will look at evangelistic preaching from the Old Testament and New Testament respectively. The sixth chapter offers four evangelistic sermons that aim at embodying the essence of our entire discussion. The final chapter offers some insights on evangelistic invitations.

4/Preaching Good News from the Old Testament

A student once confided in class that he had been a member of one church for eleven years, and during that time he never heard a sermon from the Old Testament. He said the pastor often boasted that he was a "New Testament preacher."

What a tragic indictment of the pastor's ignorance. Jesus, Peter and Paul often used the Old Testament when they taught and preached. It was the only Scripture they knew. That pastor painfully misunderstood the nature of the Bible.

To have a canon of Scripture that begins with Matthew's Gospel wrenches the Bible out of its own history. One cannot possibly read Matthew without some understanding of Israel's history as recorded in the Old Testament. Matthew's genealogy (1:1-17), his many references to prophetic utterances (for example, 1:23; 2:6, 18; 3:3, 15-16) and his allusion to Jesus as a type of new Moses require too much Old Testament knowledge to permit us to ignore that portion of Scripture. To neglect the Old Testament in deference to the New disregards nearly 60 percent of the Bible.[1] And that pastor claimed that he was ignoring it *intentionally!* We should charge him with first-degree, premeditated biblical neglect and sentence him to preach from Lamentations for the next six months.

Most of us would not proclaim such an aberrant, willy-nilly disregard of the Old Testament. In fact, evangelicals spend a good amount of time claiming how much they believe the entire Bible: "I believe the Bible is God's Word from cover to cover, all sixty-six books, including the maps!" (I have actually heard that said.) Yet how many of us neglect the Old Testament in practice? Look back over your last year's preaching and see how much of the canon you actually preached. It is not practical to preach from each of the biblical books every year. But if your survey of one or two years' worth of sermons yields an obvious neglect of major portions of Scripture, especially the Old Testament portions, perhaps the time has come to rethink your scriptural canon. Modern Marcionism might still be flourishing.

Going back to our "New Testament preacher," can you imagine what his congregation must think of the Old Testament? They couldn't possibly have high regard for such obviously neglected writings. They must think to themselves, "The preacher doesn't think it's important. Why should we read the Old Testament?" Our congregations learn as much from what we ignore as from what we acknowledge. His lack of concern for the Old Testament books tacitly, or perhaps explicitly, conveys that they lack importance and have no value. I wonder, though, if that congregation remains alone in their negative view of the Old Testament.

The designation *old* reinforces negative feelings toward it. In people's minds *old* conjures meanings such as "ancient," which conveys "antique," which leads to "antiquated," which means "irrelevant and not necessary." Antiques are nice to own, but you dare not handle them; if you break them they can't be replaced, and they're not very useful anyway. *Old* becomes synonymous with outmoded, obsolete, out-of-date, old-fashioned and fragile. Like the antique spinning wheel on Grandma's porch, it looks nice, but it doesn't work anymore. Besides, you'd better leave it alone if you know what's good for you.

Is it possible people feel the same way about the Old Testament? It has some nice stories, but it doesn't work anymore. Besides, you'd better leave it alone if you know what's good for you. Some people might legitimately ask, "What could possibly be important about stories and peoples so far removed from our culture and time? Some of its characters are colorful—Abraham, Sarah, Rebekah, Moses, Joshua, Rahab, Samson and David. They make great figures for illustrated children's Bibles, but get past their lives and you're into the barren wilderness of irrelevance. What's so important about the thirty-nine books we know as the Old Testament?"

The Old and the New Testaments have a nearly two-thousand-year history as the church's book. That fact alone says something for the durability of the Bible's witness in two testaments. However, the fact that the Old Testament has been around for a long time would not be reason in and of itself to make it a vital source of Christian theology and faith. What makes the Old Testament important to the church is that New Testament faith is rooted in and grows out of the Old Testament. The Old Testament is not ornamental or an unnecessary appendage but is an essential element of and resource for the church's faith and practice. Our understanding of the nature of the world, who we are as human beings, who we are as God's people, who God is as an active and personal player in human history is grounded in the Old Testament. Elizabeth Achtemeier deftly made the point when she said, "If we in the church do not know the Old Testament and do not teach and preach from it to our people, we leave them with no means for properly understanding and appropriating the Christian faith."[2]

The New Testament is packed with references and allusions to the Old Testament. Making correct sense of the New Testament is virtually impossible without understanding the Old. The two testaments weave a complete story of God working in the world through a chosen people. That feat comes to completion in the New Testament in the life and ministry of Jesus Christ and the development of an assembly gathering in his name, the *ekklēsia*. Jesus himself saw his ministry as a fulfillment of the prophetic oracles first proclaimed hundreds of years before his birth.

A common misconception among lay persons is that the New Testament replaces the Old. The New Testament does not supplant the Old; it brings it to completion. Jesus made this clear in his Sermon on the Mount:

Do not think that I have come to abolish the law or the prophets; I have come not to abolish but to fulfill. For truly I tell you, until heaven and earth pass away, not one letter, not one stroke of a letter, will pass from the law until all is accomplished. Therefore, whoever breaks one of the least of these commandments, and teaches others to do the same, will be called least in the kingdom of heaven; but whoever does them and teaches them will be called great in the kingdom of heaven. For I tell you, unless your righteousness exceeds that of the scribes and Pharisees, you will never enter the kingdom of heaven. (Mt 5:17-20)

Jesus showed how serious he was with the antithetic statements he made within the same sermon: "You have heard that it was said . . . But I say to you" (see Mt 5:21-22, 27-28, 31-32, 33-37, 38-42, 43-45). In these statements, Jesus heightened the traditions and Old Testament law. The New Testament brings to fruition what could only be promised in older times. Eric Rust, a former professor at Southern Seminary, was often quoted as saying that what God promised in the Old Testament he brought to completion in the New. The Old represents promises made; the New portrays promises kept.

Achtemeier argues that every passage preached from the Old

Testament should be paired with a New Testament text. Although I do not completely agree with her—because I believe Old Testament texts have an inherent value and can stand on their own—her point should be considered carefully, because she is arguing for a holistic understanding of Scripture. The Bible comes to us as a compilation of sixty-six books. Like the pieces in a jigsaw puzzle, all the books are necessary to complete the picture of Scripture. Begin to discard sections of the Bible, and you will wind up with a truncated understanding of the revelation recorded in its pages. The canon as closed by our church forebears has proven itself over time. Taking Scripture seriously means proclaiming the Bible we have in its entirety.

I have been making a case for preachers to take seriously their teaching and preaching from the Old Testament. Perhaps the "New Testament preacher" created a bigger straw image in my mind of preachers neglecting the Old Testament than it deserves. Of course, your survey of the sermons you have preached will yield the data to either support or refute the idea that we neglect the Old Testament in preaching. Most of us probably preach from the Old Testament fairly regularly, but what about evangelistic preaching? Can the Old Testament be proclaimed in evangelistic sermons? Achtemeier notes, "When our forebears in the faith finally decided on at least the basic shape of the canon, they prefaced New Testament with Old as an essential part of the gospel."[3]

Browsing around a dark, obscure section of older books in our seminary library, I came across one published by Moody Bible Institute in 1947. Its title caught my eye: *Evangelistic Preaching and the Old Testament.* I had never heard of the book or its author, Faris Daniel Whitesell. This confession is more a value judgment on my scholarship than it is on the book or its author. The book is essentially a twofold plea: "first, for more and better evangelistic preaching; and secondly, for a wider use of the Old Testament."[4] Whitesell finds endless material for evangelistic sermons in the Old Testament, as his chapter titles indicate. He offers advice on evangelistic sermons on Old Testament characters, types, institutions, doctrines, events and epochs (or ages). Then he moves from the macro to the micro with advice on evangelistic sermons on Old Testament books, chapters, paragraphs, texts and words. I'm surprised he did not also include sections on prefixes and suffixes.

Under the topic "The Values of the Old Testament for Evangelistic Preaching" he lays out sixteen reasons. Some of Whitesell's reasons are predictable; others I have covered already. Still, several others are worth citing—for instance, "the Old Testament is a human-interest book." He also says, "The Old Testament is evangelistic."[5] Whitesell is right. The Old Testament is evangelistic because it deals with faith issues: God's initiative toward human beings and our response to those overtures; the importance of relationships with God and others; the specter of sin held in tension with the possibility for forgiveness; the gifts of law and grace; redemption; God's abiding care; liberation; God's holiness in partnership with our humanness—to name just a few.

Authentic evangelistic preaching brings good news to the poor, proclaims release to captives, restores sight to those who are blind, lets the oppressed go free and proclaims the year of the Lord's favor. Jesus' sermon in Luke 4 reflects this holistic view of preaching good news. Does the Old Testament deal with any of these concerns? This chapter discusses preaching good news using the Old Testament as the basis for evangelistic sermons. Some representative texts chosen from the major sections of the Old Testament will be used for examples.

Interpreting Biblical Texts for Preaching

Before we look at some Old Testament texts, I feel it necessary to sketch an approach for interpreting biblical texts in general. This method could be used for both Old and New Testament passages, so the next chapter, "Preaching Good News from the New Testament," will also presume this basic approach.

When teaching biblical interpretation for preaching to seminarians, I get nervous about their presuming that if you follow the steps just right, as in following a recipe, then "in goes exegesis, out comes a correct interpretation." I wish it were that simple and straightforward. Biblical interpretation is a theological discipline that transcends following ordered steps. So allow the following ideas to serve as a framework rather than a set of rigid rules and regulations to follow meticulously.

1. Meet the text. Perhaps the most important part of biblical interpretation, and often the most neglected, is the interpreter's own rendezvous with the text. Because we spend so much time reading, teaching and preaching the Bible, we feel familiar with its stories, history, teaching and theology—possibly too familiar. The adage "familiarity breeds contempt" proves all too true when we come to the Bible to interpret it for preaching. How often have you approached a familiar passage—such as the parable of the good Samaritan (Lk 10:29-37)—and, because you know the story, merely read the text to familiarize yourself with details you may have forgotten? I hope I'm not the only one guilty of that practice. That routine is not interpretation; it merely yields our pet agendas cloaked under the ruse of interpreting a text. Such habits, unworthy of the high calling of Christian preaching, must be broken.

Imagine that you are meeting a text for the first time. As hard as it may be, try to approach the text as though you have never heard or read it before. What are your first impressions? Just like meeting someone for the first time, attempt not to stereotype the text. Have you ever been introduced to someone whom you decide immediately you don't like? How could you not like the person? You don't know anything about him. How can you make a judgment? She reminds you of someone you don't like. Her mannerisms, the way she smiles, the way she styled her hair, whatever, reminds you of someone else. You project those feelings you have toward another person onto this new acquaintance. The opposite can also be true. You could immediately like a person because he reminds you of someone you already admire.

We're apt to do the same thing when we interpret biblical texts. We may resent a text because it reminds us of scriptures, ideas and theology that place demands on our lifestyle; we may like a text because it sounds like it affirms our theological biases. As you read a text, jot down your first impressions, but question them reflectively to make sure you are not stereotyping or reading your biases onto it.

Rather than being a distant reader of the text, try to participate in it. As you encounter the text, how does it make you feel? A person of faith wrote the passage to other persons of faith. That group includes us. Jot down your feelings, problems, questions you have during this initial meeting with the passage. Begin looking for trouble in the text. Where do you have a problem with the text's demands or view of life? Don't jump to conclusions too quickly. Don't jot down a sermon outline at this point. And above all, don't reach for the commentaries yet. If you go for commentaries too soon, the commentator will take over and you will never have a chance to come up with your own interpretation of the text. For now, be satisfied with allowing the text to grab hold of you.

2. Read, read, read the text aloud. Some of the opening words of Revelation say, "Blessed is the one who reads aloud the words of the prophecy, and blessed are those who hear and who keep what is written in it" (1:3). This imperative can be rightly applied to all Scripture. Reading a text aloud helps us hear the texture and tone of a passage. It unlocks the words from the printed page and frees them to engage us in its event. Listen as you read, not just *to the words* but *for the world* of the text. Look for the sensory aspects of the text. What do you hear?

What do you see? What do you smell? What do you feel? Are you in the heat of the Sinai wilderness or in the chill of a Jerusalem night? Get into the physical, mental, emotional and spiritual world of the text, and the passage will come alive.

Also, read the text in different translations. If you have skill with the original languages, you should make your own translation of the passage. Preachers should own a copy of every major English translation. By comparing translations, you will have a better feel for the scope of meaning in a text. You should be aware that translations contain translator bias. All translations are inherently interpretive. Translators interpret as they translate. An example of this kind of bias is seen in the King James Version's rendering of *diakonos* as "servant" in Romans 16:1 but the translation of *diakonois* as "deacons" in Philippians 1:1 and in 1 Timothy 3:8, 12-13. Why was there a difference? *Diakonos* in Romans 16:1 obviously refers to Phoebe, "our sister"—that is, a woman. The translators' theology did not allow for female deacons, so they translated *diakonos* as "servant." Be aware of translation bias.

As you read from different translations, jot down questions, ideas or observations you are having about the text. When you finish this initial encounter, you should feel involved in the text, as if you've met an old friend for the first time. If *you* have a fresh encounter with the text, perhaps your hearers will have that same opportunity when you preach.

3. Identify the text's literary genre. Chapter two showed how form and content are interwoven. The biblical writers wrote in a variety of forms to convey the content of their messages. The obvious and primary biblical forms are historical narrative, psalm, poetry, proverb, parable, gospel, epistle and apocalyptic. These major genres also contain subforms, such as the Gospel material's sayings, pronouncement stories, speeches and miracle stories.[6] Hymns and doxologies have been identified in Paul's writings (for example, Phil 2:6-11 and Rom 11:33-

36, respectively). Knowing the form of a passage may help you understand what the writer hoped to accomplish with the text.

In preaching, fidelity to the text can perhaps be best measured if the sermon does what the text was written to do. Narrative can do some things poetry cannot; poetry can perform some feats that narrative stumbles over. The writers chose a literary form that could convey the message they had in mind. For example, biblical historical narratives provide theological insight by recalling the unfolding of events. Through characterization, plot and scenes, the writer unfolds a story. The story can address theological questions: What is God's relationship with the creation? How did the Israelites escape Egyptian slavery and wind up in Canaan? Why did Jerusalem come under Babylon's siege? Remember, biblical narrative is a theological, reflective recounting of the events that happened within a people of faith. The biblical writers were not preserving history for history's sake; historical narrative is history for the sake of theology. Knowing what the genre of historical narrative can do will make your interpretation of them more plausible.

Psalms carry the freight of meaning differently than does narrative. The psalms are not records of history, though they are certainly grounded in the history of Israel and often recall God's working in that history. The psalms are not codified laws, though they reflect the covenantal relationship between Israel and God. The psalms represent music of faith, less to be explained and more to be experienced. Biblical poetry conveys theology through parallelism, alliteration and rich metaphorical language, to name the most obvious. Where narrative leans more heavily on speaking to the intellect, poetry speaks to the heart. When we hear the words

The LORD is my shepherd, I shall not want.
He makes me lie down in green pastures;

he leads me beside still waters;
>   he restores my soul. (Ps 23:1-3)

or

Bless the LORD, O my soul,
>   and all that is within me,
>   bless his holy name. (Ps 103:1)

something inside us stirs. Psalms touch our emotions deeply
and profoundly.

Though the psalms are rooted in Israel's history, we are less
apt to think of a specific set of circumstances to which the psalm
refers. (Psalms such as Ps 137 are certainly exceptions.) The
rich metaphorical language reaches into us, and something
happens. The writers chose the genre of poetry to convey such
heartfelt emotion because, as a vehicle, poetry carries emotions
well. To interpret a psalm the same way you would interpret a
narrative violates the text's fidelity. Taking the text's form into
serious consideration is a vital step in biblical interpretation.

4. Study the text closely. At this point, a good idea is to compare
and contrast various English translations, looking for major
variations that could affect the interpretation of the passage.
Study Bibles will point out texts where the reading is problematic or whose authenticity has been questioned. The most obvious examples of such textual variants are John 8:1-11 and
Mark 16:9-20. The note in a study Bible might say something
like "Some of the most ancient authorities do not include these
verses." A less obvious passage is found in Luke 24. Suppose
you're going to preach Luke's account of the first Easter. Verse
13 obviously begins a new episode, so you feel comfortable
closing the pericope at verse 12. However, are you going to
include verse 12 or are you going to choose only verses 1-11?
You have a choice, you know. Look at the footnote in a study
Bible. The New Oxford Annotated Bible suggests that "other
ancient authorities lack verse 12." The annotation for verse 12
says, "This verse, though appearing in valuable ancient manu-

scripts, seems to be an addition to the original text of Luke based on Jn 20.3-10." Comparing translations will lead you to these kinds of variations. Because you are the interpreter writing the sermon on this text, the decision becomes yours.

Note key words and phrases in the text on which interpretation may hinge. It's a good idea to do a study of key words in the original language of the text. Using a Hebrew or Greek concordance may lead you to other places where the author used the same words and phrases. Look for strange ideas and idiomatic expressions that contemporary hearers may find difficult to understand. Try to convey these expressions in current terms. How would you phrase in modern understanding the idiom Jesus used in the following statement? "Again I tell you, *it is easier for a camel to go through the eye of a needle* than for someone who is rich to enter the kingdom of God" (Mt 19:24). A camel going through the eye of a needle appears to be impossible. This expression may have been a common idiom in Jesus' day. As an interpreter you want to make sense of such terms in today's context. Remember, for now stay away from commentaries. However, a good Bible dictionary is an invaluable tool at this point for discovering the meaning of the text.

If there are related passages, note how they illumine the meaning of your passage. For example, if you are going to preach Luke 4:18-19, you had better look at Isaiah 61:1-3. One should not interpret Acts 2:17-21 without looking at Joel 2. If you're preaching from one Synoptic Gospel, you'll want to compare and contrast what the others say. When preaching the Synoptic Gospels, be careful not to rush too quickly to harmonize the accounts. Each Gospel has an integrity of its own and does not need the other Gospels to help it out. Mark's picture of Jesus is somewhat different from Matthew's. Those who established the canon recognized the differences as a strength. If they had not, the canon would present one Gospel, a compilation of the canonical four. Each Gospel writer had particular purposes and audiences in mind when he wrote. In a way, harmonizing the Gospels creates a fifth Gospel, one that is not a part of the church's scriptural canon.

5. Examine the theological issues in the text. Never interpret a text without considering its multiple contexts. Every verse stands within the context of a paragraph; every paragraph is part of a chapter; every chapter is part of a book; every book is part of the whole canon. Every passage of Scripture should be interpreted within its specific context. If you are going to preach from a passage in Genesis, you should, ideally, begin by reading the entire book. If you are preaching John 3:16, you had better read John's entire Gospel. To do anything less is to rip texts out of their context and coerce them to say what you want them to say. Think about it. Every passage is somehow related to the whole book in which it is contained. If it wasn't, it would have vanished from the canon long before anyone read it as sacred writ. Interpreting texts within their context will help prevent proof texting.

Having a feel for an entire book gives you some indication of the author's general theological concerns. Ask the following questions as you view your text: Considering the overall theology being presented by the author, what does this text say theologically? What is the *ultimate* point of the passage? What is the theological theme of the passage? How does this theme fit into the general theme of the book? Are there other places in the book where the theme is found? How are they related to this passage? What does the text say about God? How does the passage illuminate the human condition? What is uniquely Christian about this passage? Where is the good news? These questions assume and presume that theology abides at the heart of what the biblical authors wrote. As interpreters, we want to move away from the mundane to the wondrous issues presented in the Scriptures. This point becomes especially clear for evangelistic preaching, for we defined evangelistic preaching earlier as dealing with ultimate issues.

Next, begin to think about the congregation that will hear the sermon from this text. Note the way the passage was used in its original setting. What was its relevance in its day? What did the passage *do* for its hearers? Is there an analogy between the passage and our times, a common shared experience or a contrasting one? What is the point of contact between the biblical text and your contemporary scene? At every moment of reflection and interpretation you should look for points of contact between the passage and the congregation. Recognize that when the Word engages the congregation, preaching becomes a living event.

6. Write a paraphrase of the passage. I find this step a vital practice when interpreting texts. By rewriting the passage in my own words, I can judge my understanding of the text. If I have a problem putting the text's thoughts into my own words, my comprehension of the text might be unclear. If I can't put the text into my own words, how will I preach it to a congregation?

7. Write a central idea statement. What does this text mean? Identify the text's field or scope of meaning. One passage may have several emphases or ideas (e.g., Jn 5). Make a list of possible sermon ideas based on what you discovered as you studied the text. This list should be fairly exhaustive. Select the focus or central idea of the sermon. Keep in mind that the most effective sermon does not attempt to cover too many ideas but conveys one idea with clarity. Write out, in a complete sentence, the central idea of the passage, clearly expressing the message of the text. What message or focus of the passage should this sermon communicate? This step seems difficult, but it is better for you to suffer now than for your congregation to suffer later. The central idea statement represents all the reflective and analytical work you have done with the text to this point. It is your interpretation of the text.

8. Write a function statement. How does this text mean? Determine how the passage relates to the theological intention of the author. Noting the particular genre or form of the passage may help with this step. Describe what you think the author was attempting to do—not to mean—when writing the text. What was the author's purpose in writing this text? Why did the author tell this story this way? What did he hope would happen when people read or heard the passage? What is the *function* of the passage? What does this text *do*? What does the text do for contemporary hearers?

One thing you may find helpful in deciding the function of a passage is to read around the passage as though it were not in the book. Then ask yourself this question: Now that my passage is no longer in the larger account, what *cannot* happen? If you can figure out what cannot happen when your passage is missing, then maybe you will have an idea of what it's doing there when it's put back into its rightful place. Biblical fidelity requires us to attempt to have the sermon do what the text does.

9. You may now look at the commentaries. Now that you've arrived at a personal understanding of the text, you can consult commentaries. The reason you have waited so long is that you want to be a conversation partner with the commentator and not a slave to her or his interpretation of the text. We tend to assume that commentators are experts. They have sweated over the material, living with it perhaps for years during the writing of the commentary. If we go to them too early, our attitude might be *What do I know? After all, they are the authority.* We become apt to follow their approach to the text, cajoled by their twisting of a phrase, charmed by their theological insight.

However, after you have arrived at an interpretation, you become a conversation partner with the commentator. You should use commentaries to broaden your horizons about the text, to remind you of things you have forgotten, and to inform you of insights about which you were unaware. If the commentary changes your mind about your interpretation, that's okay.

At least you had an interpretation to change. Commentaries are valuable tools but terrible masters. Allow them to challenge or affirm your understanding of the text. Always remember, the congregation called you, not the commentator, to be their preacher.

10. Move from the text to the sermon. There should be a close relationship between the central idea and function of the text, and the purpose of the sermon. Ask yourself some questions related to the sermon: As a result of hearing this sermon, what do I want my hearers to do, feel or experience? How will your hearers' lives be different having heard this sermon? If your hearers take this sermon seriously, what will your corporate life together look like? When the sermon has been preached, can you adequately answer the congregation's question "So what"? With the interpretation of the text complete, and these questions answered, you are ready to compose the sermon.

Let's now turn from general matters of interpretation to some examples of texts you might use to proclaim the evangel from the Old Testament. We will focus on three major blocks of material: Old Testament narratives, psalms and prophetic literature.

Preaching Good News from Old Testament Narratives
Evangelism begins with, is sustained by and consummates with God. Its ultimate purpose is to tell those who have never heard and to remind those who have forgotten or have taken it for granted that God, the Creator and Sustainer, desires a relationship with us. That end remains the heart of the good news. There is no better source to discover such news than the stories recorded in the Old Testament.

The witness of Scripture opens with a picture of God taking the initiative, hovering over a formless void where darkness and chaos reign, and speaking creation into existence. The chaos is harnessed and transformed by God's creative word. In a type of narrative poetry, we hear of each new day breaking forth as God delights in what is taking place: "And God saw that it was good." The anticipation builds from sky, to land and seas, to plants and trees, to the sun and moon, to fish and fowl and wild animals and livestock. As if to understand the modern adage of saving the best for last, the narrator proclaims some good news: "Then God said, 'Let us make humankind in our image, according to our likeness. . . . So God created human-kind in his image, in the image of God he created them; male and female he created them' " (Gen 1:26-27). Then God blessed them. The creation—with its fauna, fish and fowl, and its people—pleased God.

The first chapter of our canon is rich with *euangelion*. It tells of God's intentional creative acts, of the human partnership with God in sustaining the creation and the essence of good news that we are created in the very image and likeness of God. At a time when people struggle with the need to make sense out of life, when they long for meaning and acceptance, when many seem lonely and isolated, what better news than to discover that we are created in God's image. Evangelistic preaching shouts from the mountaintop that people don't have to strive to be somebody, they don't have to die of exhaustion making a name for themselves, because they are already some-body. They already have a name. They are God's children. The creation story heralds good news.

Evangelism focuses on God; but, remember, it's also about people. People never tire of hearing stories about people. When your evangelistic sermons center on life, with all its joys and pitfalls, people will listen. The Old Testament narratives are full of people: people with ambition, people who have fam-ily problems, people who make mistakes, people of faith and those who lack it, people who turn away from God, people who recognize their dependence on God. The opening chapters of Genesis portray life with all its realness. One poignant characteristic of Old Testament narratives is that they do not hide the weaknesses and pains of human life. Old Testament characters do not stand bigger than life, like mythological figures whose existence transcends that of "mere mortals."

The stories of Adam and Eve and their sons Cain and Abel bear out this fact. The first family we are introduced to in Scripture is fraught with problems. Cain and Abel prove the complexity of sibling rivalries. After Cain killed Abel, God appeared on the scene to pronounce punishing words:

"What have you done? Listen; your brother's blood is crying out to me from the ground! And now you are cursed from the ground, which has opened its mouth to receive your brother's blood from your hand. When you till the ground, it will no longer yield to you its strength; you will be a fugitive and a wanderer on the earth." (Gen 4:10-12)

Hearing the punishment, Cain pleaded with God:

"My punishment is greater than I can bear! Today you have driven me away from the soil, and I shall be hidden from your face; I shall be a fugitive and a wanderer on the earth, and anyone who meets me may kill me." Then the Lord said to him, "Not so! Whoever kills Cain will suffer a sevenfold vengeance." And the Lord put a mark on Cain, so that no one who came upon him would kill him. (Gen 4:13-15)

Only four chapters into the Old Testament, and already we have Adam and Eve banished from the Garden of Eden, and their son Cain has murdered his brother. Then, to top it off, Cain pleaded for mercy. Why would a book of faith begin by airing such problems? If I had written the opening chapters, I would have at least made excuses for the dysfunction of this first family. But the inspired writer chose not to do it that way. That's the miracle and mystery of this book.

The Bible pulls no punches. That's the problem with the Bible. The pictures it paints appear too real, too telling, too embarrassing, too problematic. Look how God acts toward

Cain. Cain pleads for mercy, and God acts mercifully toward him. God gives him a mark as a symbol of protection. It's a mark not of punishment but of grace. And God offers this sign of grace to a murderer. Now that will preach. It's just the beginning of the record of this good news that comes with God.

When preaching good news from the Old Testament look for the actions of God and the reactions of people. The Old Testament unfolds the epic of God creating for himself a people, that they might be his people and that he might be their God. The stories recounting these encounters are marked by good news. Read the stories carefully with an eye to seeing God making himself known in human history. Evangelistic sermons proclaim that revelation as good news.

Chapter two showed that the gospel was for all people. The call of Abram makes this point:

> Now the Lord said to Abram, "Go from your country and your kindred and your father's house to the land that I will show you. I will make you a great nation, and I will bless you, and make your name great, so that you will be a blessing. I will bless those who bless you, and the one who curses you I will curse; and in you all the families of the earth shall be blessed." (Gen 12:1-3)

Already, even in Abram's call, we see God acting and moving to be a blessing to all people. Now, I'm aware that first readers might not have understood the text in these terms. However, we, as Christian readers, understand texts against the backdrop of the entire canon. We recognize in this text God's initiative, not just toward one group of people but toward all people, maybe even toward us. Could it be said that here God foreshadows reconciling the world to himself? The diverse narratives of Genesis—the birth of Isaac, Jacob's chicanery, the Joseph narratives—provide rich fabric for preaching good news.

An element of the gospel is God's acting on our behalf. In Exodus, the writer recorded the acts of God on behalf of the enslaved children of Israel. Again, the stories cry out to be preached, reminding us that the gospel liberates people from slavery to service. From Moses' call (Ex 3) to the songs of praise after the people crossed the Red Sea (Ex 15), we are reminded again and again of God's intervention, as he seeks to nurture his covenant with Abraham to fruition.

Evangelistic sermons on these narratives may focus on the people involved and how frightening the prospect of liberation must have been to them. Consider how tenacious God was, and look at the people's response to that persistence. Read the stories as rich vehicles of theological truth. Remember, the Old Testament narratives endured not merely as stories for the sake of a good tale. They constituted the theological reflection, witness and testimony of people who needed the stories to make sense of their current situations. Every generation who heard and retold the stories became a part of the story. In the hearing and telling, the works of God were somehow made available again and again. I wonder if our evangelistic sermons can still make that happen?

Not long after crossing the Red Sea the people's faith came under pressure. But, again and again, the Lord's care and protection were manifested to them. Three days into the wilderness they were obviously thirsty. The only water they found was in a place called Marah, which means "bitter." *Just our luck,* they thought, *bitter water from Bitter.* And so they complained to Moses, " 'What shall we drink?' [Moses] cried out to the Lord; and the Lord showed him a piece of wood; he threw it into the water, and the water became sweet" (Ex 15:24-25). Shortly thereafter, the people complained that they had had more food in Egypt than they had in the wilderness; they were hungry. So the Lord said to Moses,

> I am going to rain bread from heaven for you, and each day the people shall go out and gather enough for that day. In that way I will test them, whether they will follow my instruc-

tion or not. On the sixth day, when they prepare what they bring in, it will be twice as much as they gather on other days. (Ex 16:4-5)

What do these narratives say about God's care and protection? What do they say about God's people? Though the texts are ancient, do they reveal something about the human condition today? Look for the way the stories unfold the developing relationship between God and the Israelites. How does faithfulness enhance this relationship? How does sin breach this relationship? How does God temper judgment and grace in these stories? Where are forgiveness and redemption shown in these narratives? Do the stories reveal a new way of making sense out of life? How do the narratives disclose who we are in the sight of God? Answer these questions, and you are on the way to preaching good news from Old Testament narratives.

Obviously, not all narrative texts are suited for evangelistic preaching. Just as in the New Testament, some Old Testament texts contain no *kērygma*. My aim is not to superimpose the gospel onto the Old Testament where it cannot be found. Nevertheless, there is more *euangelion* in the Old Testament than we have supposed. Remember C. H. Dodd's observation: "God has visited and redeemed His people."[7] The narratives from Genesis to Judges, to the exile, to the rebuilding of Jerusalem sing Dodd's refrain over and over. Give the stories a chance to speak. Who knows what good news you'll hear?

Preaching Good News from the Psalms

One role of evangelistic preaching offers people the opportunity to encounter God. The psalms suggest a vibrant, poetic picture of God, the radical nature of God's kingdom, and what living within that unprecedented kingdom means. The psalms proclaim the creative activity of God:

When I look at your heavens, the work of your fingers,
the moon and the stars that you have established;

what are human beings that you are mindful of them,
    mortals that you care for them?
Yet you have made them a little lower than God,
    and crowned them with glory and honor.
You have given them dominion over the works of your
hands;
    you have put all things under their feet,
all sheep and oxen,
    and also the beasts of the field,
the birds of the air, and the fish of the sea,
    whatever passes along the paths of the seas. (Ps 8:3-8)

Like the opening chapters of the Old Testament, this psalm
echoes the acts of Genesis. The difference appears in the personal tone of the psalm. The psalmist reflects on the immense
wonder of creation and his seeming insignificance in light of
it. Then the Genesis account must come to his mind. In a flash
the psalmist reminds himself that he is not insignificant. Human beings were crowned "with glory and honor" to participate
in dominion over creation.

Some people feel that they are insignificant, that their lives
don't matter, that God doesn't care whether they live or die. But
the gospel is meaning-making. It drastically alters common understandings. Human beings are not haphazard afterthoughts.
They have a unique place in God's sight. That good news has
transforming potential for persons who are lonely, who feel
forgotten by everyone. Psalm 8 says that in God's eyes people
matter. The psalm speaks to people's need to be loved, redeemed and sent to serve. The psalmist, having realized the
thrust of existence, ends the psalm with assurance: "O LORD,
our Sovereign, how majestic is your name in all the earth!"
(v. 9).

Another role of evangelistic preaching assures people of
God's immutable care and concern:

In the LORD I take refuge; how can you say to me,
   "Flee like a bird to the mountains;
for look, the wicked bend the bow,
   they have fitted their arrow to the string,
   to shoot in the dark at the upright in heart.
If the foundations are destroyed,
   what can the righteous do?"

The LORD is in his holy temple;
   the LORD's throne is in heaven.
   His eyes behold, his gaze examines humankind.
The LORD tests the righteous and the wicked,
   and his soul hates the lover of violence. (Ps 11:1-5)

The psalmist angrily refutes the idea that in the face of adversity one should flee to safety. "Why run when facing trouble?" the psalmist asks. He grounds his trust in the Lord's presence: "For the Lord is righteous; he loves righteous deeds; the upright shall behold his face" (v. 7). Though militaristic in tone (remember the setting of some psalms), the psalm offers a word of consolation in the face of adversity. This theme runs through the psalms. It becomes good news in any age.

The gospel is a word of healing, a reminder of God's available forgiveness, a call to redemption and freedom. What better way to proclaim such good news than to allow the psalmist to speak?

Bless the LORD, O my soul,
   and all that is within me,
   bless his holy name.
Bless the LORD, O my soul,
   and do not forget all his benefits—
who forgives all your iniquity,
   who heals all your diseases,
who redeems your life from the Pit,

who crowns you with steadfast love and mercy,
who satisfies you with good as long as you live
so that your youth is renewed like the eagle's. (Ps 103:1-5)

The *euangelion* includes the reality that human beings not only can know God but can be known by God. When I am confused about life, when I have doubts, the psalmist offers good news to me:

O LORD, you have searched me and known me.
You know when I sit down and when I rise up;
you discern my thoughts from far away.
You search out my path and my lying down,
and are acquainted with all my ways.
Even before a word is on my tongue,
O LORD, you know it completely.
You hem me in, behind and before,
and lay your hand upon me.
Such knowledge is too wonderful for me;
it is so high that I cannot attain it. (Ps 139:1-6)

Finally, a word of caution about proclamation and the psalms. Preaching the psalms takes great homiletic skill. When I see a sunset, I don't want someone explaining to me what's physically happening with the sun. To offer a scientific explanation about the myriad colors would ruin the moment. When I go to a museum to view fine art works, please don't tell me what they mean. Art exists less to be analyzed than to be experienced. I listen to Mozart, Beethoven and Bach for the pleasure the music brings, for the emotions it evokes. I'm not sure I always know what the music *means,* but I know it causes me to *feel.*

I think that's how we should approach the psalms for preaching. The psalms portray the depth of the human encounter with God. In their lines we hear words of despair (Ps 137). Some psalms offer words of comfort (Ps 23). Others provide hopeful words (Ps 121). Some psalms speak out of the intensity of existential pain and the need for God's love and forgiveness (Ps

51). The extent of the emotions portrayed in the psalms gives us a hint about how they should be preached. Help your hearers *experience* the good news they contain.

Preaching Good News from the Prophets

The prophets were preachers. If the gospel heralds the possibility of salvation, if it announces God's action in human history, if it speaks of justice, liberation, and hope, the prophetic literature exemplifies evangelistic proclamation. The gospel is about salvation. Listen to the prophet Isaiah proclaim its potentialities:

Surely God is my salvation;
I will trust, and will not be afraid,
for the LORD GOD is my strength and my might;
he has become my salvation.
With joy you will draw water from the wells of salvation. And you will say in that day:
Give thanks to the LORD,
call on his name;
make known his deeds among the nations;
proclaim that his name is exalted. (Is 12:2-3)

Lift up your eyes to the heavens,
and look at the earth beneath;
for the heavens will vanish like smoke,
the earth will wear out like a garment,
and those who live on it will die like gnats,
but my salvation will be forever,
and my deliverance will never be ended. (Is 51:6)

How beautiful upon the mountains
are the feet of the messenger who announces peace,
who brings good news,
who announces salvation,
who says to Zion, "Your God reigns." (Is 52:7)

The gospel proclaims God's moving in history. Ezekiel's prophesying to the dry bones (Ezek 37:1-14) indicates God's action in Israel's history to restore them following the devastation of the exile. The passage is a restoration text, a revival text, a word of good news for Israel:

"Therefore prophesy, and say to them, Thus says the Lord GOD: I am going to open your graves, and bring you up from your graves, O my people; and I will bring you back to the land of Israel. And you shall know that I am the LORD, when I open your graves, and bring you up from your graves, O my people. I will put my spirit within you, and you shall live and I will place you on your own soil; then you shall know that I, the LORD, have spoken and will act," says the LORD. (Ezek 37:12-14)

The prophets, like the psalmists, make God's care part of their message. Discouragement plagued the Israelites in exile. They felt abandoned by God. Evangelistic preaching often speaks to those who face discouragement at every turn. Their careers are not what they expected. Their bank-account balance always seems less than what they need just to make ends meet. Friends turn their backs, family doesn't seem to understand, and God seems absent. Do Isaiah's words say anything to their anxiety? "Those who wait for the Lord shall renew their strength, they shall mount up with wings like eagles, they shall run and not be weary, they shall walk and not faint" (Is 40:31).

The gospel calls those who hear to respond, not only on their own behalf but on the behalf of others. The glad tidings remains news of justice and righteousness, of hope and liberation. It calls for God's people to act on behalf of the forgotten and those who have no one to act for them:

Learn to do good;
seek justice,
    rescue the oppressed,

> defend the orphan,
>> plead for the widow. (Is 1:17)

> Is not this the fast that I choose:
>> to loose the bonds of injustice,
>> to undo the thongs of the yoke,
> to let the oppressed go free,
>> and to break every yoke?
> Is it not to share your bread with the hungry,
>> and bring the homeless poor into your house;
> when you see the naked, to cover them,
>> and not to hide yourself from your own kin? (Is 58:6-7)

> But let justice roll down like waters,
>> and righteousness like an everflowing stream. (Amos 5:24)

> He has told you, O mortal, what is good;
>> and what does the LORD require of you
> but to do justice, and to love kindness,
>> and to walk humbly with your God? (Mic 6:8)

I also pointed out that the gospel doesn't always make sense—that it sometimes echoes a difficult or unbelievable word. The Israelites probably wondered how good could come of their circumstances. They faced a wilderness between themselves and their beloved Jerusalem. What good could possibly happen? Isaiah proclaims the impossible:

> The wilderness and the dry land shall be glad,
>> the desert shall rejoice and blossom;
> like the crocus it shall blossom abundantly,
>> and rejoice with joy and singing.
> The glory of Lebanon shall be given to it,
>> the majesty of Carmel and Sharon.
> They shall see the glory of the LORD,

the majesty of our God. (Is 35:1-2)

It makes no sense. How can a wilderness be glad? How can desert bloom? Wildernesses exemplify the absence of joy. Deserts mark the barrenness of life. How can they sing? Because they see God! The poetry of Isaiah proclaims the radical eruption of all creation at the sight of God. Is not the gospel about turning the worldview upside down? In God's kingdom, even deserts rejoice and blossom. This message tugs at the core of *euangelion*.

Perhaps the most poignant example of grace that comes to the undeserving, of the unbelievable love of God, of the radical nature of good news, comes near the end of Hosea:

How can I give you up, Ephraim?
How can I hand you over, O Israel?
How can I make you like Admah?
How can I treat you like Zeboiim?
My heart recoils within me;
my compassion grows warm and tender.
I will not execute my fierce anger;
I will not again destroy Ephraim;
for I am God and no mortal,
the Holy One in your midst,
and I will not come in wrath. (Hos 11:8-9)

If it were us and our kids, we would disown them: "You had your chance, now you're on your own. Fend for yourself." The good news is that God doesn't act that way. God views life differently. Luckily for us, the gospel isn't dependent on human initiative.

Summing Up

For those who have eyes to see and ears to hear, the Old Testament contains much good news. It deals with matters of faith like God's initiative toward human beings and our response to those overtures, the importance of relationships with

God and others, the specter of sin held in tension with the possibility for forgiveness, the gifts of law and grace, redemption, God's abiding care, liberation, God's holiness in partnership with our humanness. But the Old Testament does not offer a complete picture of the *evangel*. That realization presents itself in the New Testament, to which we now go.

5/Preaching Good News from the New Testament

*M*ost preachers need little, if any, prodding to preach sermons from the New Testament. Ministers regularly preach from the New Testament, especially when preaching evangelistic sermons. An apologetic like the one I presented for preaching from the Old Testament seems moot and superfluous here. I've never heard anyone claim to be an "Old Testament preacher" to the neglect of the New. If preachers slight the Old Testament in their preaching, it's probably because they have emphasized the New.

The New Testament presents an obvious source for Christian preaching. Its collection of twenty-seven books tells the story of Jesus of Nazareth as God's promised and anointed one. The New Testament's writings show the development of the early church and its enthusiastic movement throughout the known world. The books give a glimpse into the life, tensions and triumphs of the first faith communities as they struggled to understand what it meant to be followers of Christ.

The New Testament describes a ragtag bunch of fishermen, tax collectors, artisans, carpenters, homemakers, businesswom-

en and men "turning the world upside down" (Acts 17:6) for
the sake of Christ. We preach the New Testament because it
records the foundations of our faith, the possibilities of kingdom life, the dilemmas of discipleship and the realness of being the church in the world. In this litany, the echoes of good
news already call out to us. We sense intuitively what was not
readily apparent in the Old Testament—the gospel character
of the New Testament. *Euangelion* is blown throughout its
pages.

In what follows, we consider specific passages from the New
Testament in terms of evangelistic preaching. Our survey includes some obvious texts that by their very nature and substance demand evangelistic preaching. The harvest may prove
more fruitful, though, as we consider some passages less obviously bent toward evangelism but whose word for the church
rests in the heart of the gospel. We will look at some texts from
each of the four major literary forms in the New Testament:
Gospel, church history (Acts), letter or epistle, and apocalyptic
(Revelation). The scope of this book allows us only to scratch
the surface of texts that one could preach evangelistically.

Preaching Good News from the Gospels

The Gospels tell *the* gospel. They present the good news of
Jesus Christ. They describe his birth, baptism, ministry of teaching, preaching and healing, crucifixion, resurrection and ascension.

The Gospel writers were not just storytellers, though their
stories demonstrate an astute narrative ability. The Gospel writers were theologians. They infused the narratives they wrote
with intentional design and purpose. They recalled the life of
Jesus of Nazareth and recorded the events to communicate
theological truth and import to their readers.

The Gospel writers were preachers, interpreting the life and
ministry of Jesus Christ in theologically significant terms. Jesus

was not another prophet heralding a future messianic hope; he signified the very Christ of God, making God's kingdom available to all who would respond.

The Gospel writers were evangelists. They heralded good news. Life is different now because Jesus Christ lived, died and lives again. Relationships take on new light because of the Christ event. A kingdom ethic supplants conventional wisdom, morals and ideals. The Gospel writers proclaimed the good news by telling Christ's story.

Of course, each of the four Gospel artists painted the picture of that story differently. No two preachers preach the same sermon from the same text. My sermon on John 3:16 will sound familiar, but it will not be the same as your sermon on John 3:16. Likewise, because the Gospel writers were good theologians and preachers, they sermonically interpreted the events of Christ's life in ways that spoke to their particular audience's needs and concerns. Mark's Gospel lacks a birth narrative and postresurrection appearances. Luke's Gospel contains only an abbreviated version of the Sermon on the Mount, yet it includes such stories not found in Matthew or Mark as Zacchaeus's climb up the sycamore tree and Cleopas and the other disciple's encounter on the Emmaus road. Matthew quotes many Old Testament passages to show Jesus as the fulfillment of prophecy. Neither Luke nor Mark found such validation essential. John rearranges the chronology of certain events—for instance, Jesus' cleansing of the temple—for theological emphasis.

These examples point out that the Gospel writers had specific theological concerns and purposes for presenting the material the way they did. In fact, we may discover the theological message of a particular Gospel by looking for what that writer included or omitted in comparison to the other Gospels. As you preach selected Gospel passages, keep in mind that each Gospel has its own theological concerns. Therefore each passage should be considered in its fuller context, namely the entire Gospel of which it is a part. The above prolegomena lays a foundation for preaching good news from the Gospels.

Matthew 1:18-25: God is with us. Herein lies Matthew's account of Jesus' birth. Matthew foreshadowed Jesus' life in the opening verse by saying, "Now the birth of Jesus the Messiah took place in this way." The Messiah is born; God's anointed one, the Christ, has entered human history. Though Joseph had already decided to divorce Mary quietly, an angel spoke to him in a dream, describing the unique nature and ministry of the child: the child is from the Holy Spirit, his name is to be Jesus, and he will save his people from their sins (vv. 21-22). Matthew showed prophecy's fulfillment by quoting Isaiah 7:14: " 'Look, the virgin shall conceive and bear a son, and they shall name him Emmanuel,' which means, 'God is with us' " (v. 23).

An evangelistic sermon on this text can focus on God's inexplicable breaking into human history. God has always been an actor in history. When Jesus was born, however, God took on human flesh and personally became a part of that history. The incarnation signaled God's unique personal intervention into human life. Life changed drastically because of this intervention. Help your hearers see how radical life is when you proclaim Emmanuel, "God is with us."

Some people believe God to be a distant, uncaring force. But Matthew's text shows that God can no longer be perceived as an absentee landlord with little or no concern for people's lives. Many people, even some who have spent their whole lives in church, don't understand that Jesus Christ is God. The doctrine of God and the doctrine of salvation hinge on the incarnation as the unique event in all of history. A sermon that announces this proclaims good news.

Matthew 20:1-16: Surprised by grace. Matthew's account of the laborers in the vineyard is provoked by Peter's caustic question to Jesus, "Look, we have left everything and followed you. What then will we have?" (19:27). The vineyard story is framed as if with bookends, with Jesus' words about the first being last and the last being first; bookending often provides an interpretive clue to a passage's theological significance.

Jesus tells that the kingdom of heaven is like a vineyard owner who went to the marketplace early in the morning to hire laborers. At six in the morning he hired the first workers and promised to pay them a day's wage. Throughout the day he hired others, including a group whom he employed when there was only an hour left in the workday. When the owner beckoned the manager to pay the workers, he told him to pay first those whom he hired last. They received a full day's wage. Those who worked the whole day were angry because they received the same as those who worked only an hour. The owner reminded them that he had done nothing wrong. They had received the agreed-upon wages; nevertheless, he wanted to be gracious to those who had worked only one hour.

Where's the good news in this text? A sermon could focus on several *euangelion* themes in this passage.

First, like the landowner, in kingdom life God looks for people. The initiative is with God, not with us. God's acting intentionally as Redeemer and Sustainer hints the gospel's presence.

Second, what we receive from God is not based on merit—how long we work, how committed we are, not even how faithful we are. God's gift to us is *grace*. That's hard to hear in a culture raised on the idea that you get what you pay for. We are a you-get-what-you-deserve people. Fortunately, when it comes to theology we do not get what we deserve. God meets us with grace greater than our sin.

Finally, the passage shows that God's grace comes as paradoxical surprise. Those who worked only an hour were surprised by what they received. So were those who worked all day. Our God is a God of surprises, longing to bless us when we least expect it, wanting to broaden our horizons when we least want our horizons broadened.

"So the last will be first, and first will be last" (v. 16), Jesus said. Sometimes the gospel ruptures our sensibilities. It does not conform to a human system of values. Even that stark reality is good news.

Mark 2:13-17: He ate with sinners. This passage contains Mark's account of the call of Levi. Levi collected taxes—not a popular occupation anytime, anywhere. When Jesus accepted his invitation to dinner, some surely said, "Not a good move, Jesus. Your reputation, you know!" When the religious leaders saw him eating with societal outcasts, they decried him: "Why does he eat with tax collectors and sinners?" The good news of Jesus' response leaps from the page: "Those who are well have no need of a physician, but those who are sick; I have come to call not the righteous but sinners" (v. 17).

An element of the *euangelion* that I have emphasized is God's movement on behalf of the forgotten and neglected. Religious elitism was not only a first-century malady. Many church people would be angry with Jesus if they saw him eating with "those people." Again, the gospel becomes a two-edged sword. For those who feel neglected by society, including the church, this word is a word of inclusion: you are welcomed into God's kingdom. For the self-righteous, this word becomes an intrusive invasion into comfortable religion, an invasion relished by the gospel.

Mark 8:34—9:1: A troubling gospel. Although the gospel is good news, it is not always easy to hear, even for disciples. The gospel is not cheap news or demand-free. This passage from Mark provides the preacher an excellent source for an evangelistic sermon about discipleship. Here Jesus lays out his demands for would-be followers: denying self, taking up a cross, saving one's life by means of losing it, losing one's life by means of saving it. Here is where the gospel sticks its finger in the face of uncontrolled relativism. Jesus demands more than intellectual assent to religious dogma. The good news insists that a new worldview is on the scene, a new order of thinking, a new way of making meaning, a new way of treating people, a new way of glimpsing who we are in the sight of God.

If you choose to preach this text, be careful that your sermon does not turn into a moralistic tirade of *shoulds, oughts* and *musts*. That approach takes the easy way out. Show what life will look like when your hearers deny themselves. Describe what it feels like to take up a cross to follow Christ. Be experiential by telling them the story of someone who did just that. Tell them about a family who saved their lives by losing it, like the couple who could have "enjoyed life" once their kids were grown but decided to become the parents of two children orphaned by a devastating house fire. Jesus did not talk in esoteric theory; he spoke in terms of experiential theology. Help your hearers see that when they encounter Christ life can never be the same again. That's also part of the gospel message.

Luke 5:17-26: Stand up and walk. Chances are good that you will not find many contemporary, twentieth-century people talking about sin. It's just not a very popular subject. People cringe at the mention of the word. No politically correct, well-educated person would discuss the subject. They might talk about psychological maladjustment or behavioral problems or a flaw in character development or major personality disorders or mistakes, but sin? Not a chance. People think that if you don't mention the word, then sin no longer has influence over their lives. People's unwillingness to call sin by name—a reality even present in our churches—dupes them into believing that technology, medicine, modern economic theories and a score of other cultural advances will ultimately solve the hideous crises in the world. Yet without sounding anachronistic, evangelistic preaching can warn that sin remains an ever-present, destructive evil in our midst.

Like many Gospel stories, this one is found in all three Synoptic Gospels (see also Mt 9:1-8 and Mk 2:1-12). The accounts read quite similarly, though Luke added that the people listening to Jesus came from "every village of Galilee and Judea and from Jerusalem" (v. 17). This parenthetical statement might reflect Luke's concern for the universality of the gospel—what was happening was for all people (Lk 2:10).

When preaching this text, one could certainly focus on the faithfulness of those carrying the paralyzed man to Jesus for healing. But the tension in the text flares when Jesus said to the one paralyzed, "Friend, your sins are forgiven you." The scribes and Pharisees called Jesus' words blasphemy because only God could forgive sins. Modern sensibilities would likewise call Jesus' words blasphemy, but for another reason—because he talked about sin to someone who was paralyzed. In either case, the gospel cannot be held down by our presuppositions. The forgiveness of sin swirls throughout the *euangelion*. Jesus forgives sin—a word of good news even when people don't want to talk about it. An evangelistic sermon on this text might have some, even in church, saying, "We have seen strange things today."

Luke 15:25-32: The other prodigal. Chapter 15 of Luke's Gospel contains three parables about lostness: a lost sheep, a lost coin and a lost son. In the next chapter of this book I present Raymond Bailey's evangelistic sermon on the earlier and more familiar episode about the lost son from Luke 15:11-24, traditionally known as the parable of the prodigal son. Bailey rightly suggests that this parable should be called the parable of the two lost sons. It is to the second son's story that we turn our attention—and for good reason.

Many people may identify with the younger brother's dilemma—a wayward life brought on by selfishness and greed, experiencing the pit of despair, realizing one's fallacious ways, then seeking forgiveness and restoration, only to be redeemed beyond the wildest of expectations. It's a great story. It reverberates with good news. It's an excellent text for a sermon to unchurched people who have never seen the vastness of God's love.

But some people won't identify with the younger brother or his follies because they, like the elder brother, grouse at the father's seemingly unwarranted benevolence. If the prodigal's story speaks effectively to unchurched people, the elder brother's story provides a basis for an evangelistic sermon to church people. Remember, one aspect of preaching the *euangelion* reminds the church of grace they may have forgotten. Preaching good news to the church helps disciples grow in faith.

A sermon on this text should show how Christians can become resentful about blessings given to others. The elder son came in from working the field and heard music and dancing. "What's going on?" he asked a servant. "Your brother has come, and your father has killed the fatted calf, because he has got him back safe and sound," replied the servant (v. 27). When the elder son heard the good news, he became furious.

If you have served a church for any length of time, you have met some "elder brothers." They are difficult people to serve. They think the church owes them for all their years of faithful ministry. They expect special favors because of their unblemished efforts on behalf of the kingdom. Help them to hear the gospel in this passage: "Then the father said to him, 'Son, you are always with me, and all that is mine is yours. But we had to celebrate and rejoice, because this brother of yours was dead and has come to life; he was lost and has been found' " (vv. 31-32).

John 4:1-42: A remarkable gospel. Like the story of Jesus and the man at the pool of Beth-zatha, the encounter of Jesus and the Samaritan woman provides rich material for several sermons heralding good news. The gospel breaks down barriers created by human misunderstanding, prejudice, bigotry and racism. Jesus asked the woman for a drink. Notice how captive she was to the rules she had heard all her life: "How is it that you, a Jew, ask a drink of me, a woman of Samaria?" John's parenthetical explanation of her comment says it all: "Jews do not share things in common with Samaritans" (v. 9). She had been taught well that Samaritans had no dealings with Jews and that women did not fraternize with men at the well. Jesus' willingness to talk with her (vv. 10-26)—literally to discuss theology with her—exemplifies the gospel's liberating message.

The encounter overwhelmed the woman because Jesus knew everything about her—including her apparent current adulterous situation—and still treated her as if she were somebody. He talked with her. He listened to her. He acknowledged that she indeed was a person, a reality her culture intentionally ignored. The gospel reclaims personhood. It reminds people that God loves them and cares about them. A sermon on this text can remind contemporary hearers that in God's eyes they are somebody.

Following her encounter with Jesus, the woman returned to the city and shared her story. Because of her testimony, many Samaritans from that city believed in Jesus. Again, a hallmark of the gospel: a most unlikely candidate became an effective evangelist. Many people feel inadequate, unqualified, even unworthy to speak a word on God's behalf. The woman told her story; she shared her testimony and many believed. Help your hearers claim their story in Christ. It may be some of the best preaching you will ever hear.

John 7:53—8:11: Gospel of the second chance. Though this account is not found in many ancient manuscripts—therefore its originality to John's Gospel is questioned—it bears the evangel so poignantly that it calls out to be preached. In an evangelistic sermon on this text be sure to point out the rigid way the scribes and the Pharisees understood the law. In their zeal to maintain the law, their righteousness turned into unrighteous indignation. The text contains a warning for modern listeners here—

preachers and congregations alike. For example, the church needs to address the rampant relativism plaguing American society, including American Christianity. In so doing, however, we must be careful that our zeal for truth is not corrupted into personal vendettas or self-serving agendas. Otherwise the cure will be worse than the disease.

The religious leaders wanted Jesus to uphold their stringent understanding of the law. Anyone who had spent just a little time around Jesus knew that he would not disappoint them. He did not allow their desire for the letter of the law to escape its own indictment: "Let anyone among you who is without sin be the first to throw a stone at her" (v. 7). Soon the accusers were gone, having succumbed to the weight of their own wish for righteousness. "Woman, where are they? Has no one condemned you?" he asked of her. She said, "No one, sir." Then she encountered the gospel of the second chance. Jesus said, "Neither do I condemn you. Go your way, and from now on do not sin again" (vv. 10-11). Many who sit in church pews Sunday after Sunday find themselves condemned under the weight of past and present sins. Preach from this text that Jesus gives them a second chance.

Preaching Good News from Acts

The Acts of the Apostles recalls the development of Christianity during the approximately thirty-year period following the death and resurrection of Jesus Christ. In Acts, Luke continues the story of his Gospel, beginning with the resurrection and ascension of Jesus and ending with the apostle Paul preaching the gospel in Rome "without hindrance" (28:31). Acts follows the narrative form of the four Gospels. It is the genesis story of the church and the account of the gospel's spreading from Jerusalem to Judea and Samaria, and ultimately to the ends of the earth. Though the church in Acts bears little resemblance to the organized, even bureaucratic church of today, the contemporary church finds its roots in the community of faith described there. Acts is the story of the Holy Spirit empowering believers—the *ekklēsia*—to carry the good news to the world. When you preach evangelistically, you continue the heritage of carrying the gospel of Jesus Christ to the world.

Acts 2:44-47: A transformed community. Saying that the events of the Day of Pentecost were life-changing is the quintessential understatement. With power from the Holy Spirit, a timid band of disciples became confident evangelists. Peter preached an evangelistic sermon, calling people to repent and to be baptized in the Lord's name. Because of the sermon and the testimony of the other disciples, about three thousand persons became Christians that day.

Again, the gospel announces the present manifestation of God's kingdom, a kingdom that requires a different way of understanding life and making sense of relationships. Acts 2:44-47 bears witness to these radical demands and requirements. The text is Luke's summary statement following the events of Pentecost. Any sermon on this text should place the passage clearly in that context.

The believers demonstrated a unity that obviously captured Luke's attention. If having "all things in common" followed customary practices, he would have overlooked it. The believers' newfound relationships with Christ and with each other moved them in outlandish ways: "they would sell their possessions and goods and distribute the proceeds to all, as any had need" (v. 45). Though this practice may not have had widespread acceptance outside the Jerusalem church (see 5:4), it's obvious that these Christians experienced much joy through sharing all they had.

Luke also records that day by day they spent time together in the temple (not just for an hour or two on Sundays). They ate meals together that were characterized by gladness and generosity. They spent time together praising God. Luke indicates the possibility that many people looked upon this band of believers with great favor. The gospel had obviously transformed these people's lives. Their daily routines were dictated by the fellowship they now experienced in Christ. They began to live together the way they would live eternally in God's kingdom.

Now, if you start preaching that Christians should sell their possessions and distribute the proceeds to any who have a need, folks may get upset and offended. But did you notice something interesting about this text? It doesn't seem that anybody told them to sell their possessions or to share all things in common. It appears that their actions naturally grew out of the good news they had received. I wonder what would happen in our churches if we began to act on the gospel we have received. I wonder what we would do.

Acts 16:25-34: A simple question, a penetrating response. Familiar texts should be a part of your repertoire for evangelistic sermons. Of course, when preaching familiar passages, be sure not to neglect the reflective and exegetical study prescribed in the previous chapter. Even passages that you have preached before can yield new fruit when you have eyes to see and ears to hear.

This passage offers you the opportunity to preach a sermon with a twofold purpose: for Christians, you can focus on the faithfulness and readiness of Paul and Silas to offer the gospel anytime; for unchurched people, you can lead them to ask the jailer's question for themselves. If you choose to begin the passage with verse 25, as I have suggested, provide some background information as to why Paul and Silas found themselves jailed in the first place. You can offer a brief summary of verses 11-24 before reading the passage in worship, or you can summarize the unfolding incidents in the introduction of the sermon.

As with all narrative texts, the sermon could describe the

events as they unfold. In doing this, do not presume omniscience for yourself; it is a trap into which preachers often fall. For example, be careful not to read too many details into the happenings, such as the kind of hymns the two prisoners were singing or the reason for the earthquake (the text gives absolutely no hint about either) or a scientific explanation of why the doors opened and everyone's chains were unfastened. Inquisitive minds may want to know this information, but they remain moot points in the text. Care must be taken not to read our twentieth-century issues onto a first-century text. You could, however, spend time dealing with the jailer's attempt to kill himself, because the text indicates some degree of motive: "since he supposed that the prisoners had escaped" (v. 27). This incident may lead you to describe the desperate situations that drive people to desperate acts. The gospel addresses such desperation.

The crux of the passage is the jailer's question, "Sirs, what must I do to be saved?" If we probe the jailer's query too deeply, it raises more questions than it answers. Paul and Silas spent no time pondering the basis for the question. Notice how they answered: "Believe on the Lord Jesus, and you will be saved" (v. 31). For them, no matter the reason or motivation for the jailer's question, the answer was the gospel—believe on the Lord Jesus and be saved. Without discounting the severity or motivation of your hearers' experiential questions, offer them the gospel, in all its simple complexity—believe on the Lord Jesus.

Preaching Good News from the Letters

Twenty-one books of the New Testament are in the form of letters. The authors wrote to particular congregations to address particular situations. Though the letters were written primarily to early Christian congregations, several were written to individuals. In general, the letters provided instructions in the faith, gave direction and advice concerning questions that arose, admonished believers when disagreements happened and challenged them to live fully in Christ. Reading them, we catch glimpses of the earliest Christian congregations and the struggles they faced in living their faith in the world.

The New Testament letters have a sermonic character, which makes them ideal as a source for preaching. Unlike the Gospels, which communicate theology through narrative, the letters appeal to direct discourse. With a sense of urgency and conviction, the writers urge their readers to take seriously the demands of the gospel they have received. Warnings to the Corinthians about immorality, the challenge given to Philemon to treat the slave Onesimus as a Christian brother, James's insistence on putting faith into concrete examples of Christian compassion—all the letters urge a new ethic, a new way of looking at life, a new way of making meaning based on the gospel. To these churches the gospel was not a religious system, a kind of handbook to be consulted now and again; it was a way of life wrought by the Holy Spirit and made possible through the life, ministry, death and resurrection of Jesus of Nazareth, the Christ. The New Testament letters exude the gospel.

Galatians 5:1: The liberating gospel. By choosing a single verse, I appear to be violating my own admonition of ensuring that a complete thought unit be used as a preaching text. Usually a single verse lacks adequate context. But this verse summarizes and climaxes Paul's letter to the Galatians, so we're on safe ground preaching it. Of course, familiarity with the entire correspondence is necessary to understand the thrust of this text.

Galatians 5:1 commences the conclusion of the letter, in which Paul provides ethical responses to the idea of Christian freedom. In short, the letter deals with whether Gentiles must first become Jews before they can become Christians. Certain teachers had come to Galatia and were saying that the Galatians must keep the Mosaic law along with faith in Jesus Christ. Paul viewed such teaching as heretical and a desertion of the unique freedom made possible in Christ: "For freedom Christ has set us free. Stand firm, therefore, and do not submit again to a yoke of slavery."

These words echo Jesus' sermon in the synagogue at Nazareth (Lk 4). Jesus said that his ministry was going to be characterized by liberation and freedom; Paul says it has happened. Paul recognizes the liberating nature of the gospel because he has experienced its emancipation firsthand. Freedom, the watchword of the gospel, is available in Christ. The evangel breaks into the world with liberating power. The kingdom of God has entered history. God has saved us from our own oppression, removed the shackles of our sin and set us free. "Why then," Paul asks, "would you submit yourselves again to slavery?" That question can be the basis of an evangelistic sermon on this text.

Some cautions should be kept in mind when you are preaching this text. The situation in contemporary churches does not exactly parallel that being faced by the Galatian Christians. The question whether one has to follow the Mosaic law to become a Christian has long been answered. But the church in every age faces analogous threats to freedom. There are churches today shackled by rigid religious legalism. Rather than following the Spirit, they are still dominated by the letter of the law (2 Cor 3:6). Examples of such unquestioned legalism might include the exclusion of divorced persons from full participation within the Christian fellowship and the subjugation of women and their exclusion from leadership positions in church. Such legalistic stances keep the freedom available in Christ from taking root. Allow your sermon to make clear the freeing notion of the gospel.

Another caution centers on choosing this text merely as the centerpiece for a sermon on freedom in general. I have heard this text used several times as the basis for sermons preached on the first Sunday of July. The preachers act as though it was a small step from the freedom of this text to the freedom Americans enjoy. Before long the patriots of 1776 and Jesus sound as though they were counterparts in the same revolution. Actually, though, freedom in Christ, the freedom of which Paul speaks, has no nationalistic boundaries. This text is not about being free to participate in democratic processes or being able to live where we choose and to lay out our own destinies. In reality, the freedom wrought in Christ produced a revolution of infinite proportion. Freedom in Christ ruptures the shackles of sin for eternity. Though Americans value their freedom highly, it pales compared to the freedom we have in Christ.

Galatians 5:1 proclaims that for freedom Jesus Christ has set us free, free to live in God's kingdom as fellow heirs with Christ. This message is a potent word for those outside Christ. Help seekers understand what authentic freedom in Christ means. Be sure to maintain the integrity of the gospel by making clear its demands and responsibilities. Freedom is such an important concept for Westerners. Help those who are not Christians see that ultimate freedom can be gained when we submit to the lordship of the One who makes real life possible.

This text also contains good news for the church. Christians need to be reminded again of the liberating nature of the gospel. After all, such was the motivation for Paul to write these words in the first place. Evangelistic sermons are not just for the unchurched; the church starves that does not hear the gospel preached.

1 Peter 2:1-10: Becoming God's people. Another text that speaks a word of good news to both citizens and foreigners to the kingdom is this passage in 1 Peter. The first three verses call for Christians to strive for maturity after ridding themselves of malice, guile, insincerity, envy and slander. These are inappropriate behaviors for God's children. This is followed by words

of invitation in verses 4-6: "come to him" and "let yourselves
be built into a spiritual house." Peter contrasts those who believe and those who do not. He then speaks some of the most
affirming words in all of Scripture for the church: "but you are
a chosen race, a royal priesthood, a holy nation, God's own
people" (v. 9).

Every congregation eventually questions its reason for existing: an inner-city congregation is blighted by suburban flight;
a staff minister admits to sexual impropriety with several church
members; a congregational fight is fueled by powerful families;
leaders are unable to cultivate new volunteers; people are experiencing burnout due to legalistic adherence to mundane
rituals. Coming to church becomes a chore. The joy vanished
long ago. Now the single motivation for existing as a congregation is mere habit. A sermon based on 1 Peter 2:9-10 may be
the good news some congregations desperately need to hear.

Remind your listeners that God chose them. Myriad images
can be cited to incarnate both the joy of being chosen and the
pain of not being chosen. Some will remember choosing up
sides in school sports. Being chosen mattered. Peter reminds
the church that they are a chosen people, a royal priesthood,
God's very own people. Your evangelistic sermon should show
that they have been chosen for a reason: to "proclaim the
mighty acts of him who called you out of darkness into his
marvelous light" (v. 9). Our chosenness in Christ motivates us
to become a blessing to others and to proclaim the good news
so that they may discover that Christ has likewise chosen them.

Help your hearers recognize that once they were not a people, but now they are God's people; once they had not received
mercy, but now they have received mercy. For a church flound-
ering in self-doubt that message may be the good news that will
motivate new commitment to the cause of Christ.

James 1:22-27: Doing the gospel. The gospel disrupts our comfortable world. It won't allow us to meander aimlessly with our

Christianity tamely on a leash. Whether we are modern seekers and worshipers enjoying the comfortable setting of a contemporary church (no three-piece-suit preachers here) or traditional church people (clinging to gold-leafed, color-coordinated King James Version Bibles), the gospel will get in our face. That's just like God, isn't it? When we think we've got God all figured out, just at the point when good news seems domesticated, it turns on us like a disloyal friend. We feel this way because we misunderstood the nature of its friendship. We believed that the gospel was friendly because it sounded our theological concerns. It voiced our agendas—whether we are liberal or conservative, we could make it sound like us—so we preached it with great zeal. Then we come across a passage like this one, which pulls us from a warm pew, drags us back down the long aisle and pushes us out the door into the real world. We ask, "What do you think you're doing? Who do you think you are?" It curtly responds, "The gospel, of course!"

"Be doers of the word, and not merely hearers," James bids his readers (v. 22). The gospel is more than a word to be heard, it's life to be lived. Jesus and the disciples tended to the physical and spiritual needs of people. They saw the gospel as a message for body, mind and spirit. An evangelistic sermon may urge a congregation to supply hungry people with food. It may challenge people to roll up their sleeves and get their hands dirty building a house for a homeless family. Preach a sermon on this text, and urge your congregation to empty their pockets for somebody else's children. That's what the gospel says in this passage: "Religion that is pure and undefiled before God, the Father, is this: to care for orphans and widows in their distress" (v. 27). It's not an easy word to hear. It will challenge your best preaching. But it is, after all, the gospel.

If you choose to preach this text, be sure to provide some concrete ways your congregation can do the word. To speak of Christian service in general terms will gain some intellectual assent, but it will not move hearers from the sanctuary into the marketplace. Tangible needs present themselves to most Christians every day. What your sermon must do is motivate them to see and respond to those needs. Also, help your hearers recognize that you are not merely advocating secular social work in Christian garb. The gospel's unique message speaks to physical and spiritual needs. The church doing ministry is the church presenting Christ, the church spreading the gospel.

Preaching Good News from Revelation

If a slighted book exists in the New Testament, Revelation would surely claim the title. Its strange language, bizarre visions and cryptic symbols seem so enigmatic that most preachers opt to scout out friendlier sermonic terrain. By its nature, the book attracts such a variety of interpretations that congregations are exposed to everything from the sublime to the absurd. Charts and graphs, timetables and chronologies, hints and hunches as to what or who will be the beast this year abound.

Jim Blevins, an authority on Revelation, pleads for "sound and sane" preaching from this important book: "The book has a positive message of hope for people facing despair and persecution. Revelation has a timeless message which transcends the first century and the struggles of the Christians within the Roman empire."[1]

Revelation uses apocalyptic as its genre to communicate its message. Apocalyptic—from the Greek *apokalypsis,* meaning "uncovering, disclosure or revelation"—was a familiar literary form to first-century Jews and Christians living throughout the Roman Empire. As Tom Long points out, writers of apocalyptic didn't start the day saying, "Let's see. Shall I speak poetically today, or narratively, or . . . ? Ah yes, I know, I shall speak apocalyptically—lightning, sulfur, the moon dripping blood and all that."[2] Writing apocalyptically was an intentional choice provoked by grievous circumstances.

People facing persecution, religious intolerance or myriad other acute crises understood the cryptic language and images of apocalyptic and therefore could make sense out of the literature for their situation. Their enemies, the perpetrators of injustice or persecution, were ignorant of the codes, so if they came across an apocalyptic book it seemed to them bizarre gibberish. If they had known that the literature was written to instill hope, to provoke perseverance, to proclaim a victory yet unseen, surely they would have destroyed the writings. That was one reason the literature was written the way it was, to protect it from destruction.

Another reason for writing apocalyptically was the genre's ability to transcend time and space. Whereas John wrote Revelation specifically to first-century Christians enduring persecution, probably under Domitian—and with no concern for twentieth-century musing about the mark of the beast or the identity of the whore of Babylon—the book's message of hope under duress transcends temporal bounds. This fact makes Revelation a timeless message of good news for the church.

Since Revelation's message heralds God's ultimate victory over the powers of evil, sin and death through Jesus Christ, it provides a fitting conclusion to the Old and New Testament. It announces the pinnacle of good news: Jesus Christ is Lord and reigns forever, alleluia. Come Lord Jesus!

Revelation 1:9—3:22: Letters to the seven churches. Because Revelation is divided into a prologue (1:1-8), seven major sections (1:9—22:5) and an epilogue (22:6-21), one approach to preaching the book would be to do a series of nine sermons covering each of these major sections. Admittedly, such an undertaking would focus on highlights rather than details, but your congregation would at least have a panoramic view of the entire book. When one is studying a book as detailed as Revelation, examining the bark on every tree invites monotony and boredom, and the larger thrust of the book vanishes among technicalities.

A different method would be to preach a series of sermons from all or, based on your particular congregational situation, selected letters to the seven churches. For example, the church in Ephesus was affirmed for its patience yet indicted for abandoning "the love you had at first" (2:4). Likewise, the church at Laodicea had become lukewarm in its faith and relished its seeming independence: "for you say, 'I am rich, I have prospered, and I need nothing' " (3:17). As I mentioned before, churches can lose their sense of direction and purpose. Love of God is measured by faithfulness to the complete message of Christ; a church's actions, as well as beliefs, measure fidelity. The evangel challenges churches today to regain direction in Christ. If you preach using these troubling examples, be sure to be specific in citing places where you see you and your church falling short. Notice how each of the seven letters cites specific instances to praise and blame.

Mention of the Laodicean church prompts a word of caution. Evangelistic sermons based on Revelation 3:20 abound. The passage is familiar: "Listen! I am standing at the door, knocking; if you hear my voice and open the door, I will come in to you and eat with you, and you with me." The sermons portray Jesus Christ standing at the locked door of an unbeliever's heart. Even paintings based on this verse show a door lacking a knob on the outside. The sermons plead that the door must be opened by the needful, unregenerate sinner inside. In fact, the letter was not written to a lost person; it was addressed to an apostate church. The image is that of a church door, not an unbeliever's heart. Those who shut the Christ out were not unbelievers but Christians.

Being faithful to texts sheds new light on the good news that begs to be preached from them. Words of hope and comfort, along with words of challenge and accusation, reveal the gospel in this section of Revelation. Insightful preachers will find here an evangelistic word—though sometimes an intrusive one—

from the Christ to their churches.

Revelation 5:6-14: Eternity today. Here the heart of New Testament *euangelion* calls out. In a vision John sees, between the throne of God and the four living creatures (representing all of creation), a Lamb. First-century Christians knew the identity of the Lamb; twentieth-century Christians are urged to join the choir. The four living creatures and the twenty-four elders sing to the Lamb (vv. 9-10). Then untold angels join the chorus singing, "Worthy is the Lamb that was slaughtered to receive power and wealth and wisdom and might and honor and glory and blessing!" (v. 12).

Revelation's essence is thoroughly liturgical. Long rightly notes that the book of Revelation "wants the reader to see what is happening in that other place, that heavenly realm."[3] Worship breaks out around God's heavenly throne:

> The hymns they are singing in heaven as they worship, the prayers they are praying, the creeds they are confessing are the very same hymns, prayers, and creeds employed by the church on earth. In other words, while the earthly church sings "Worthy is the Lamb" with a racing heart and a fearful lump in its [throat] . . . the church victorious in heaven sings harmony on the very same hymn.[4]

Perhaps a sermon on the joy of already participating with the saints in praise of God would demonstrate the nature of the gospel for a congregation. I have noted how concepts of salvation often create an image of a heavenly insurance policy. Some view heaven in the same way they peruse a travel brochure of the Bahamas. The sites look great, the water's inviting, the food's exotic, the temperature's grand, the price is right. Wouldn't it be nice someday to go there? But we don't have to wait. When we sing and pray and proclaim in worship, we are surrounded by a cloud of witnesses who sing and pray and proclaim with us: "Worthy is the Lamb!" The gospel is *now* news.

Revelation 21:1-7: No more tears. The gospel proclaims hope to those who have lost hope. It brings comfort to the comfortless, consolation to the lonely, victory to the defeated. Ultimately the good news offers life to those who are dead. With this text as a source for an evangelistic sermon, you can proclaim that the end of life's novel is known. God is victorious. The reality of Emmanuel comes to full realization (v. 3). God dwells with his people, and he, God's very self, will wipe every tear from their eyes. Death will be a faint memory of a distant pain. Mourning and crying are forgotten. Preach so your congregation hears God speak:

It is done! I am the Alpha and the Omega, the beginning and the end. To the thirsty I will give water as a gift from the spring of the water of life. Those who conquer will inherit these things, and I will be their God and they will be my children. (vv. 6-7)

Summing Up

Please allow the above examples to serve as catalysts for your own discovery of other evangelistic preaching resources in the New Testament. Once you have enlarged your understanding of the gospel, you no longer need to choose only the texts that specifically sound evangelistic. Rather than containing a limited number of passages from which evangelistic sermons could be preached, the New Testament radiates *euangelion*.

6/Practice What You Preach: Four Evangelistic Sermons

*T*his chapter contains four evangelistic sermons that model the issues and ideas we have been discussing. Two sermons are based on Old Testament texts and two on New Testament passages. Two of the sermons, one in each section, were composed by me. One sermon is by William Willimon, dean of the chapel and professor of Christian ministry, Duke University Divinity School, and the remaining one is by Raymond Bailey, professor of Christian preaching and director of the National Center for Preaching at the Southern Baptist Theological Seminary, Louisville, Kentucky. The chapter concludes with a brief evaluation of the sermons and some reflective questions for analyzing evangelistic sermons.

The Day of the Lord
by William H. Willimon[1]
Amos 5:18-24

This is Sunday, the Lord's Day. This is the day when we worship. That's what I first taught at Duke Divinity School, worship.

I am sort of an expert on worship. Proper behavior on Sunday, the Lord's Day.

Which means that I have some definite opinions about how worship ought to be. I have an image about how worship is when it is done right, and I expect that you have an image, too, of how worship ought to be. That's why many of you are here on this Lord's Day, because, in your opinion, Duke Chapel does it right. Here is your idea of "good" worship.

I have my own pet peeves and prejudices about "good" worship. For instance, I'm not much on chatter before the service. We put a note in the bulletin, at the top of the first page, telling you not to chatter during the prelude, but sometimes you still do. I don't like that. Another thing—I don't like preachers with "stained glass" voices. Know what I'm talking about? "A blessed welcome to you this blessed morning. Now let us all rise and turn to hymn 435." I don't like that. Children's sermons? I don't like them. If the preacher wants to star on "Uncle Bill's Fun House," let him do it at a time other than Sunday. "May we pray?" I don't like that either. What if some Sunday somebody shouted, "No, you may not"? It's "Let us pray."

Plastic flowers (tacky), all male ushers, good-looking preachers—I don't like them. And I'm sure that, if you were doing the talking, you would have your list. (Preachers with Southern accents, cute remarks from the pulpit, homiletical attacks on the dean of students . . .) You don't like it.

Yet how often have we asked, What does God like about worship? What does God expect from a Sunday morning? Back to my liturgical thoughts: A primary purpose of our Sunday praise and prayer is *location*. We don't just worship anywhere. We come to a place, a location, a special location. On Sunday morning we get our bearings, so to speak, locating ourselves within a sometimes chaotic and confusing cosmos. Perhaps that is why we build our places of worship bigger, costlier than they need be. It takes four football players to move Duke Chapel altar.

It became the custom in the church to build our buildings always oriented the same way, facing east. Even when, as with our chapel, we're facing sort of north, we still call it "east."

Worship locates us. When you're a student, far from home, this chapel can be a place where you are able once again to be embraced by the familiar and the predictable. Everything may be cut loose in our lives, but when we come in on Sunday, things are again tied down, just where we left them at home, comfortable, reassuring, linked to the past.

Sunday is therefore the day to affirm ("I believe in God the Father Almighty, Maker of heaven and earth . . ."), to confirm ("This is my Father's world: I rest me in the thought . . ."), to order in grand procession the eternal verities.

In church, furniture tends to be heavy, bolted down, fixed, immovable. We have a rule in the chapel. If you get married here, you have to take it, in the words of our wedding guidelines, "as is." No moving, rearranging or dislocation permitted here.

And yet sometimes, as we are busy affirming, confirming, ordering, locating, there is a dislocating intrusion. When Sunday regularity hardens into stifling stability and Sunday is a day only for reiteration of royally approved definitions of reality and worship is but the embodiment of the establishment, sometimes there is dislocating intrusion.

Such, I think, is today's word from the prophet Amos. We have begun, as we usually do, with ourselves, asking what we want from worship. Now what does God want? What is God's definition of "good" worship?

"Woe to you who desire the day of the Lord!" Why do you want to get close to God, to celebrate a day with the Lord? "It is darkness, and not light." To come to God is to flee from a lion only to be embraced by a grizzly. Or to arrive breathless into the safety of your own house, there to be bitten by a rattler. Here is darkness, not light.

Amos is talking about the Day of the Lord. That hoped-for, prayed-for day when God would at last come down and be with God's people, that day when the presence of God would no longer be something high, far off and distant, but here.

"Maranatha!" ("Come, Lord Jesus") is probably the earliest of Christian prayers. Come, Day of the Lord. Come, be with us.

"You want that day?" says Amos. Be careful! That day is gloom, not light, a bear, a poison snake.

And then Amos hears God speak some of the most terrifying, dislocating words in the Bible. "I hate, I despise your feasts, and I take no delight in your solemn assemblies." Bring your offerings up to the altar? "I will not accept them, . . . I will not look upon [them]. Take away from me the racket of your songs; to the melody of your pipe organs I will not listen."

God says, Your worship makes me sick. The smell of your offerings, your sweet incense rising into the rafters, nauseates me. Your lovely four-part harmony hurts my ears. Take it away!

Go ahead, says God, sing your little songs—I don't like your kind of music. Preach your sermons, pray your prayers—my ears are closed.

What does God want? What is "good" worship? How are we supposed to celebrate properly the "Lord's Day"?

You know the words: "Let justice roll down like waters, and righteousness like an ever-flowing stream."

There may be gods, there may be religions, for whom worship is but the beating of a drum, the ringing of a bell, the burning of sweet incense, or the repetition of high-sounding words. Israel's religion, Israel's God, is not one of them.

You know what I love on Sunday morning? A joyous chorus from Handel; a clear trumpet, sounded from our organ, by Purcell; to see that silver cross lifted and moving in stately procession down that aisle; coat-and-tied, chaste sophomores attentively seated on the second row. That's what I like.

"You know what I love on the Lord's Day?" says the Lord.

"Justice rolling down like Niagara, righteousness flowing like the Mississippi, that's what I like," says the Lord.

In the exodus, Moses is sent to Pharaoh to ask for a few days off for the Hebrew slaves so "we can go out in the desert and worship our God."

Moses continues to plead, "Let us go so we can worship our God." Pharaoh continues to refuse. Ten plagues and much pain later, Pharaoh consents. "Okay, Hebrews, get out of here and don't look back until you are someplace other than Egypt."

At last they are free to worship. Well, they get out in the desert, free, ready to worship God. But how? Nobody has ever worshiped this God before, at least not for a long time. They've forgotten how. Are there directions? Anybody got a copy of the hymnal?

Then God takes Moses up on the mountain, while the people await further rubrics. "I am the Lord your God, who brought you out of the land of Egypt," says God in a voice like Charlton Heston, "so that you might worship me."

"Yes, yes," Moses replies, "but how are we supposed to do that? Do you like gospel music or are you more into Gregorian chant? Do you like the King James Version or the *revised* Revised Standard Version?"

"You know what I like?" says the Lord. "I like the kind of worship where you shall have no other gods before me. You do not kill. You don't steal. You don't commit adultery. That's my idea of a good time on Sunday. The ethical linked to the liturgical." Moses found it is a disrupting experience to worship this God!

What we want is Sunday as a time of stability. Our ministers become managers of conventional definitions of reality; our liturgies, an embodiment of the establishment. There is the King on the throne, here are we, all in a line of bolted-down pews. Sunday is about eternal continuity of the known, old world.

Yet here comes a disruptive, prophetic word, a linguistic assault upon the presumed, fixed, royal world. Amos's contemporaries longed for a "day of the Lord," assuming that day would be in continuity with present arrangements, assuming the present arrangements are God's arrangements, that current social, political, economic configurations are divinely ordained.

No, says Amos, in words that shatter the presently legitimated order. No. On the Lord's Day, the world ends. The granite walls of the post office, city hall and even your chapels melt under the blast of God's breath. That's your Day of the Lord. The established, royal world cannot tolerate prophetic speech about the end of the world. Liberal academic religion, so comfortable and adjusted to present arrangements, only mildly uneasy with the status quo, purges apocalyptic talk of the end from Sunday morning. For if a prophet named Amos or Jesus ever stood up and announced the end, that would shatter the present order. The end of an old world has power to evoke a new world; termination leads to evocation.

"I hate, I despise your feasts, . . . the noise of your songs. . . . Let justice roll down like waters, and righteousness like an ever-flowing stream." How are we doing, Lord?

An evening with the Durham Bulls is more racially, culturally integrated than a Sunday morning in Duke Chapel.

What we have here is a prophetic, linguistic assault on the establishment, poetic delegitimation of present configurations of power. But we don't want prophets. We want ministers who are managers of consensus, temple functionaries who scurry around the altar on Sundays in a desperate attempt to keep our known world intact, reassuring us of the eternal stability of the status quo, "God's in his heaven: / All's right with the world."

The known, fixed, royal world is disrupted by prophetic, poetic speech about the end of the world.

A couple of years ago I was the host for Will Campbell, acerbic but brilliant Baptist novelist and prophet. It was Sunday;

we were walking up the walkway through the woods toward the chapel, my favorite way to approach the chapel on a Sunday. Bells were ringing, early Sunday sun glistened off the chapel tower. It was glorious, beautiful. I was proud, and felt that this visitor was probably impressed. He's from Nashville.

Then, as the trees cleared and the chapel rose before us in all its stately grandeur, I heard Campbell mutter, "Humph! He's come a long way from Bethlehem."

It's All Hebrew to Me
by Craig Loscalzo[2]
2 Kings 18:17-37

You'll have to excuse me this morning. I'm not feeling so well. You see, I'm having a major midlife crisis. I'm not sure what's bringing it on. Maybe it's because people are offering me their seats in waiting rooms. My sixteen-year-old son just got his driver's license. I hyperventilate every time I give him the car keys.

Maybe it's because of TV. TV is strange today. There used to be just three networks. I grew up on NBC, CBS and ABC. Now it's NBC, CBS, ABC, MTV, VH1, CNN, TNN, QVC, KET, HBO, TMC, TNT, BET. There are forty-two channels in Louisville alone. And none of them carry my favorite show—*All in the Family.* I haven't seen an episode, not even a rerun, in seven years. The new shows make little sense to me. Who ever thought of giving a zip code its own weekly series: 9021 . . . what? For a while there was a show called *Twin Peaks.* I watched it a couple of times. I never understood any of it. Who was Laura Palmer anyhow? I'm having a major midlife crisis!

Whatever happened to US Keds? Nobody wears sneakers anymore; I always wore sneakers. Now it's Nike Air Jordans, Barkleys, Pippens, David Robinsons, Air Huaraches. They say "Just Do It." I would, but I can't afford it!

Whatever happened to the local diner—split-pea soup, liver and onions, and homemade lemon meringue pie? Now it's all fast food: Golden Arches, Whoppers, Blizzards and that overweight, middle-aged Dave trying to convince me that I'll really like Wendy's hamburgers. Their ads say I can have it my way. Well, then, let me have my diner back!

I find myself thinking about retirement, reflecting that Woodstock wasn't so bad after all, wondering why I can understand Bob Dylan but not rap music, and dreading the day when I'll have to wear one of those remote-control emergency things— you know, "I've fallen and I can't get up." I'm having a major midlife crisis.

What makes it worse is that the church is also having a midlife crisis. The church is having trouble deciding what it's going to be in the postmodern world. The church isn't sure how it's supposed to react to contemporary society or how it's supposed to speak to today's culture.

It probably all began in the sixties. People blame everything on the sixties. That's when the church faced hippies. Then came yuppies, and baby boomers and busters, and who knows what's next. Today's culture is driven by an "ethic of self-fulfillment."[3] The seventies was called the "me generation," and the eighties was the "my generation." Who knows what the nineties will be called?

We live in an "instant" world. I think it all began with the most horrible of inventions, instant coffee—yuck. How could anybody fall for that Folger's switch-at-the-last-minute stuff? And then instant mashed potatoes—hang wallpaper with them. The parade of instant never ends—instant oatmeal, instant grits, instant loans, the fax machine bringing instant mail, instant relationships, instant prayer, instant discipleship. If it's not immediate we won't wait. My son actually asked why microwave ovens take so long.

Technology and postmodern culture are synonymous. Computers make our work easier, faster and less frustrating (so the advertisers say!). Culture is obsessed with gadgets. Everybody has a cellular phone. Don't forget the remote control for the TV. If my wife and I ever need marital counseling it will be because of that remote control. She can change that channel so fast that I wonder what Oprah Winfrey is doing on *Star Trek: The Next Generation.*

I fear some churches will buy into the new technology lock, stock and barrel. Can you imagine a church using one of those automatic telephone computers: "Hello, this is First Baptist Church. We are personally concerned about you and those you love. If you have a touch-tone phone and are lonely and need someone to talk to, press 1; if you are having marital problems, press 2; if you want to confess some sin, press 3. And don't miss our annual bazaar and garage sale this Saturday morning." I'm not sure how that all plugs into the gospel.

The list goes on—you know it well: materialism; a drive for more leisure time; the loss of institutional loyalty, including loyalty to denominations or the church; the loss of meaningful traditions.

How can the church be the church in the face of so many obstacles? How can we lead the church into the twenty-first century? While struggling with these questions, I came across an article by Walter Brueggemann. In it he provides a fascinating glimpse and interpretation of 2 Kings 18—19.[4]

Jerusalem is under siege from the Assyrian king Sennacherib. In the preceding verses, King Hezekiah tried to appease Assyria, hoping that Sennacherib could be bought off. But Sennacherib wanted Jerusalem, nothing less.

The king of Assyria sent three messengers and a large army to negotiate the surrender. They stood outside the gate of the city and called for King Hezekiah. Hezekiah sent three of his officials to meet with the Assyrians. The dramatic scene begins with a conversation at the wall of the city.

The Rabshakeh—Sennacherib's chief of staff—began negotiations: "Ask Hezekiah the basis for his confidence? Does he
think that words can win a war? If he's relying on Egypt's promises for help, he's got a long wait. If he's relying on the Lord,
he'd better think again!"

Hezekiah's envoys were angered that the Rabshakeh was
speaking Hebrew: "Please, speak to us in Aramaic; we understand it. Don't speak to us in Hebrew. The people will understand what you're saying and will become so frightened that we
won't be able to negotiate."

Indignantly the Assyrian spoke in Hebrew even louder so
that those on the wall and behind the wall could hear: "Hear
the word of the great king of Assyria. Hezekiah won't be able
to help you. Don't listen to him about God's help. Make peace
with me and you'll live abundantly. Hezekiah misleads you by
saying, 'The LORD will deliver us.' Whose gods have delivered
their countries out of my hand, that the LORD should deliver
Jerusalem out of my hand?"

The argument at the wall is a familiar one. It is a metaphor,
says Brueggemann, of the conversation taking place between
the church and culture.

The Assyrians argue for their ideas, their presuppositions
about what the world is like. Theirs is a rational worldview, one
that makes much sense to them. The power of military numbers
should overwhelm Judah. Assyria is the stronger kingdom; they
will surely prevail. This is their mindset: "You can't rely on
Egypt. Don't bother listening to Hezekiah, the Lord can't deliver you. Listen to us, we'll make things right." The idea is *go
along to get along.* "Don't make waves. Open your eyes to the
reality of our force." In other words, we are the dominant power, so you might as well adopt our plan.

Sadly, that is always one of the options for the church in
dealing with the prevailing culture: accommodate and adapt in
order to survive. After all, a domesticated Christianity is no

threat to culture.

Tex Sample, in his book *U.S. Lifestyles and Mainline Churches,* says that the tendency to accommodate Christ to culture is not new in church history: "Sallman's head of Christ turned Jesus into an Anglo with movie-star looks. Bruce Barton's *The Man Nobody Knows* made Jesus a Rotarian. . . . The New Age makes him a channeler, a guru, or a guide. Athletes turn him into a jock, and rock lovers proclaim him as superstar."[5]

In the book *All God's Children and Blue Suede Shoes,* Kenneth Myers has problems with Christians who accept cultural images by sanitizing them with "Jesus language."[6] So following Coca-Cola, Jesus "is the Real thing." And following Pepsi, Jesus becomes "the right one, baby, uh-huh." Gold's Gym becomes "God's Gym."

Whoopi Goldberg plays Sister Mary Clarence in the movie *Sister Act.* An ex-nightclub singer, she poses as a nun in the witness protection program. Because of her performance skills, she is put in charge of the choir and turns a sleepy congregation into vibrant worshipers with such hits as "Nothing in This World Can Keep Me Away from My God." Even the pope is impressed. Myers says that Christians have accomplished being of the world, but not in the world.

Books like *The Frog in the Kettle* and *User Friendly Churches* offer some insights for understanding the baby boomer and baby buster generations and how churches can reach them.[7] Marketing the church must be done with integrity and authenticity. I hear ministers talking about all the latest ways they "meet the needs of the boomers." The real danger in these methods is that church becomes a cafeteria line where people pick and choose parts of the gospel that fit their lifestyle. Christianity cannot be consumer-driven.

Accommodation in the biblical story is really noticeable in the Rabshakeh's use of Hebrew rather than Aramaic in the conversation at the wall. You might say, as I did, "Hebrew,

Aramaic, what's the difference? It's all *Hebrew* to me."

Here Aramaic is the language of commerce, the language of diplomacy. It's the language he should have used for such negotiations. Hebrew is the language of faith. It's the language that members of the community of faith use to speak to each other. It's the language they use to speak about God. It's the language they use to speak to God. It's covenant language. Brueggemann warns that when the imperial powers are at the wall and use the language of faith, the people of God are in trouble.

The church needs to hear that warning, especially when the wall between church and state becomes threatened. When politicians try to sound like preachers, the church is in trouble. When the government couches its policies in the church's language, the church is in trouble. We are only deluding ourselves into believing that political powers really have the best interests of the church at heart. Politicians look for votes and will stand at the wall and speak Hebrew if that's what it takes. We are only kidding ourselves if we believe that the power of politics will advance God's kingdom. Such is solely the task of the church. God is not a Democrat or a Republican. God's reign transcends political affiliations. We will never adequately communicate the gospel to our culture if we don't understand that.

The Assyrian spoke Hebrew for political gain. It was for no other reason that to win Israel's favor, and ultimately Israel's submission. But Hezekiah warned the people not to answer. Maybe they couldn't answer, muses Brueggemann, because they didn't understand the fake Hebrew spoken by one who didn't know the power of the language of faith.

At the wall, Assyria disregards Judah's trust in Yahweh; it is unreasonable and makes no sense. But, behind the wall, inside the city, there is another conversation taking place. A conversation by a different set of people with different values. In the conversation behind the wall, no one questions Yahweh's power over against the power of Assyria. Hezekiah sends for the prophet Isaiah and describes the situation. Isaiah's response is quick and to the point: "Relax, Hezekiah. Don't be afraid of Assyria. God is in control" (2 Kings 19:6). That's Isaiah's good news for Hezekiah.

Behind the wall a different understanding of life is at work. Here is where the community of faith speaks the language of faith, a language that makes no sense to those at the wall. It is behind the wall that the church speaks of redemption and fellowship, of Eucharist and communion, of baptism and forgiveness, of hope that transcends material possessions, of joy in self-denial, of the expectation of life after death. It's behind the wall that such conversations make sense.

Please don't hear my call for a conversation behind the wall as a call to separation. Some Christian thinkers call for the church to survive separated from the world. Much like Anabaptists, they appear to call for a sectarian understanding of the church in the world.

Neither the accommodation of culture nor separation from culture is a viable alternative for the church. Brueggemann calls for an authentic Christianity that is *bilingual.* People of faith must be able to talk at the wall, because the Assyrians are conversation partners and they must be taken seriously. They will not go away.

However, unless there is another conversation behind the wall, in another language, about another agenda, Judah will submit to Assyria's demands, and the church will fail at being light to the world. In Tom Long's words, the church must be the language school for the kingdom of God. It's behind the wall, in church, where we learn the language and the customs and the stories of the kingdom, the good news stories. It's our practice of this behind-the-wall language that makes it possible for us to proclaim the gospel to those outside the wall. And proclaim the gospel we must. It is our mandate. It is our call.

"Don't be afraid of Assyria," said Isaiah. "God is in control."

In the face of rabid relativism, political correctness, religious fanaticism, the church probably is having a midlife crisis. Under such duress, what better news to hear: Don't be afraid; be the church. God is in control.

You Can Go Home Again
by Raymond H. Bailey
Luke 15:11-24

The fundamental questions of human existence do not change. Scientific advancement and technological progress alter the forms and style of our lives, but the fears and compulsions which haunt and motivate us are the same ones that plagued our ancestors. The dissatisfaction with plenty that shattered the garden paradise, the jealousy of Cain, the insecurity of Jacob, the stupid priorities of Esau, the vanity of the builders of Babel, the greed of the Napoleons of the world and the cruelties of the Hitlers—not to mention the little fears, insecurities and power drives of every one of us—are universal.

The authority of Scripture is demonstrated time and again as it reveals to each generation the universality of human foibles and the power of love. One New Testament scholar observed about the parables that we do not interpret them but they interpret us. So it is with us and with this familiar story of a young person's search for meaningful existence.

We have a tendency in our study of Scripture to accentuate the negative lessons rather than the positive ones. This story begins with a very important lesson about a fundamental privilege of being human. At some point in his adolescence the central figure became aware of his individuality—his right of choice. An awareness of that special gift of God that only humans, of all the creatures of this world, possess. Animals are not free to change their pattern of life or to choose between different lifestyles or different sets of values. They are ruled by instinct and environment, but humans can control their instincts and have the power to change their environment—for good or evil.

The son had the right to choose his way of life. That is part of what it means to be human. He could reject sonship and search for his notion of freedom and independence. It is the will of God that it should be so.

Many today, grieved by the wrong choices of loved ones, wish that it were otherwise—that God had not made us free. Some prefer authoritarian religions because they do not want to be responsible for their decisions. Some parents deprive their children of part of their humanity by making them emotional cripples—unable and unwilling to choose, *sheltered* but also *denied*. The individual who is not free to choose, who is not free to make personal decisions is not a whole person. She or he is incomplete.

If we do not have the freedom to reject God, then we do not have the freedom to accept Him. It is the will of God that everyone be free to choose to trust or not to trust.

The younger son exercised his human freedom and chose to try it on his own. He wanted to be *independent*, demanded his inheritance and struck out on his own. Perhaps it was a necessary step to self-discovery. One theology has suggested that we move through the stages of dependence and independence to interdependence in relationships.

At first the world seemed friendly enough. He was received with open arms. His youth, his energy, his carefreeness, his wealth made him a popular guy. How much better it seemed than home. No one moralized to him. No one criticized his health habits, his way of dress. No one told him when to go to bed or how long his hair could be or mocked his earring. No one asked of him more than what they could carry away in their hands.

It was only when he was all used up that he realized he had been used at all. How many people have given their lives to a business, an industry, a sport, a club, a political party, or a habit only to wake up alone one day—unwanted, with nothing to show for their service but a gold watch, a plaque or broken health? How many strong and talented young athletes have enjoyed the glory of being sought after and courted by a score of colleges and wake up the morning after a serious injury to find that no one's really interested anymore? How quickly the names of might-have-beens or even yesterday's heroes are forgotten. Today's heroes are tomorrow's forgotten.

Famine came and friends faded away. Famine always comes in one form or another—physical loss, emotional deprivation or even natural aging. One modern paraphrase reads "He began to feel the pinch." At one time or another, each of us feels the pinch and "no one gives us anything."

Much of the history of the world is implied in this story of the exploitation of a human being. How friendly the world looks when you have something to give, and how hostile it becomes when there is nothing left to give—to the merchant, the bank, sometimes even your own family, the mate who no longer finds you attractive, the greedy child. Where were all his drinking buddies, where were all his dancing partners and business acquaintances when he found himself in the pig pen?

In Arthur Miller's play *Death of a Salesman,* Willy Loman, after a lifetime of selling on the road for a firm, pleads with his employer for a nontraveling assignment. He simply can't handle the tough life of the road. His boss is already thinking of restructuring and tells the worn-out old man that he is no longer needed at all because after all "it's a business . . . and everybody's gotta pull his own weight."

How it hurts to realize that those with the strong handshake and the ready smile bestowed them upon a customer, a client, a citizen rather than a human being. The world asks, "What's in it for me?" It does not give—it trades. God asks, "What's in it for you?"

Jesus tells us that the man was hungry, tired and dirty, but surely the pain was not all physical. His humiliation was total, and how he must have hated himself. The proud self-confidence that had propelled his rebellion and driven him into the world had been blown away. Nothing hurts more than self-loathing and the sense of personal failure. When physical strength is gone, when your knowledge is not the latest, when you're no longer the prettiest—what then? How agonizing to discover that the commodity upon which your relationships have been built is no longer marketable. The feeling is even more acute when there is the faint remembrance of how it was at home, of what we were and of what we might have become.

"I am my father's son . . ." What does it mean to be "my father's" child? It means that I am worth something to somebody. Even in the lowest depths of human degradation when I have nothing of value to offer to anyone, I am of value to someone. Because I am a child of God I have worth and dignity. Paul Tillich said the task of the church is to get people to realize that "they are accepted." While we were yet sinners Christ died for our sins. Every human at some point in his or her life experiences fear, alienation, and loneliness, but not everyone realizes what it means to be God's child. The lost man remembered home.

You can go home again. Home, says T. S. Eliot, is "the end of all our exploring . . . to arrive where we started. And to know the place for the first time."

The attitude of the model father of this story is something to behold. I can't believe that a single day passed by that he did not think about the son who was gone, did not hope for a word from him, did not pray for his success and happiness, did not go down the road and strain his eyes peering into the distance hoping to see the boy, who must now be a man, coming home.

The parent's pain was the powerlessness of the God who makes his children free and responsible. The child must come home of his own volition. When he did come home, what a reception and celebration! This celebration was not predicated upon his appearance or his wealth or even a contrite spirit. It was freely given without measure or reservation, as is the love of God.

Freedom is not a place. It is a state of mind and being, a self-concept of what it means to be the pinnacle of creation. Perhaps only when all the façades and illusions are stripped away by loss, pain or discovery do we realize what it means to have God for a parent and Jesus for a brother.

Fred Craddock tells a poignant story of a childhood game of hide-and-seek. He found the perfect place to hide from his sister. The counting was over, the search had begun and he gloated in his secret hiding place. "She will never find me. She will never find me. She will *never* find me." He suddenly realized that in his lonely place, he would never be found. From under the porch where he had hidden, he stuck out a toe just enough to be seen. Do we really want to hide in our lonely far country?

An Idle Tale?
by Craig Loscalzo[8]
Luke 24:1-11

I have a feeling I know why you're here this morning. Some of you came for the music. Certain hymns make so much more sense when we sing them on Easter Sunday morning—"Christ the Lord is risen today, Alleluia!" and "Up from the grave he arose, with a mighty triumph o'er his foes." And I like how we sing Easter music—with a lot of joy and enthusiasm, like we're going to wake up the dead. Some folks might not be crazy about church music the rest of the year, but they seldom complain about Easter music. If you're here for the music, I don't think you'll be disappointed.

Some of you are here because you're visiting family or friends and they invited you to come to church. Easter is a great time to spend with family and friends. It's special to experience worship with those we love. I hope your visit is a fun one.

I'm not naive. I know some are here under just *a little* duress. "After all, it's Easter Sunday," goes the plea. "Please go to church with me." Or maybe the request was a bit more persuasive—"It's Easter Sunday, and whether you like it or not, you're going to church." "Are we having fun yet?" they mutter to themselves.

There might even be some here because you're a bit curious about this whole crucifixion/resurrection obsession we Christians have. You want to see what it's all about. Some are here to see who else came. Some are here because you're always here.

But I wonder, if we really understood Christ's resurrection, would any of us *dare* come to church? Especially on Easter Sunday!

The sun had just begun to illuminate the morning sky. They had stood at a distance and watched him die. They had followed him from Galilee, to Jerusalem, to the place called The Skull, and to the tomb where he was buried. Now, on the first day of the week, some women, and only some women, were going to the cemetery to complete what they were not able to finish on Friday. When they arrived, they found the stone rolled away from the tomb—they went in. His body was gone. They were dazed and perplexed. Two men in dazzling clothes stood beside them. In terror, the women bowed their faces to the ground. The men said to them, "Why do you look for the living among the dead? He is not here, but has risen. Remember how he told you, while he was still in Galilee, that the Son of Man must be handed over to sinners, and be crucified, and on the third day rise again."

They did remember Jesus talking about that. They went back to Jerusalem and told the others what had just happened to them. But the story seemed to them . . . an idle tale. The disciples did not believe them. The women were dazed and terrified. The disciples thought their story was an unfounded, groundless lie. And the passage ends.

Where's the Easter music, pealing with shouts of "Alleluia" and "Christ the Lord is Risen Today"? Where's the pageantry we Christians have come to expect at Easter? We're left with frightened women and accusations of lies and deceit. What kind of Easter scene is this?

Well, those who crucified Jesus had a lot of problems with him. Jesus wouldn't comply with their wishes. He wouldn't conform to their plans. He kept preaching good news to the poor. He incessantly talked about liberating those who were captive and giving sight to those who were blind and freeing those who were oppressed. *Just who is he talking about?* they thought. "Just who does he think he is?" they said.

Jesus wouldn't submit himself to their theological view of the world. He wouldn't succumb to their narrow views about God. He kept talking about the inauguration of God's reign—as though he were some kind of Messiah. They *had* to do something. When you are the religious establishment, you can't maintain your credibility with someone like Jesus going around undermining it all the time. They had to act. So on Friday, they took matters into their own hands. They got rid of their problems on Friday.

Think about it. Jesus hanging on a cross is not going to be any trouble to anybody. "We've got him right where we want him," they said: "No more talking about loving your enemies now, Jesus. No more of this going the extra mile now, Jesus. No more doing lunch with Zacchaeus now, Jesus. No more pointed stories about lost sheep and lost coins and lost kids now, Jesus."

Jesus had been a problem to them for a long time. You could say it began when a ragtag bunch of shepherds tromped into Bethlehem babbling about angels and glad tidings. When Jesus was twelve, he gave the teachers in the temple fits. Then there was that sermon in Nazareth: "Today this scripture has been fulfilled," he said. "Today!"

"This guy's going to be trouble," they said. "All this talk about good news and liberation and God's kingdom." He was becoming a real problem to them. But not any more. Jesus hanging on a cross is not going to be any trouble to anybody. They got rid of their problems on Friday.

On Sunday, the women were terrified and the disciples were hiding out—saying that empty-tomb stories and risen-Jesus stories are all just big lies. Is it possible . . . they recognized their problems were just beginning?

Jesus lying in a tomb is not going to be any trouble to anybody. The women went to the tomb to embalm their dead friend. The disciples are hiding out, thinking about how they'll put their lives back together. They're nostalgically reminiscing about what it was like to be with Jesus: "Remember the good times we had with Jesus—the strolls along the beach, the nice lunches with the crowd. Remember his nice stories? You know the ones about the lost sheep, and the lost coin, and the lost kids. Don't forget the one about that friendly Samaritan. Remember how he used to talk about how things could be, how they *really* could be?"

Now they have to face the possibility that their problems are just beginning. Jesus lying in a tomb is not going to be any trouble to anybody. But begin talking about a resurrected Jesus—all heaven might break loose. This kingdom of God stuff might start happening. We might start loving our enemies. We'll start having to go the second mile. We're going to have to intervene when we see injustice perpetrated against the poor. We'll be yearning for righteousness if we're not careful. We're going to have to start practicing this good news stuff—this gospel Jesus proclaimed. When you stop to think about it, this risen Jesus is a real problem!

And people come to church on Easter Sunday thinking they can enjoy the music or visit with family and friends or maybe even tolerate another Easter sermon. Not with this risen Jesus roaming around! This risen Jesus is much too much of a problem to allow that. His gospel is dangerous, risky, messy business. It expects you to roll up your sleeves and get your hands dirty for somebody else's children. It won't allow you to sing "In the sweet by and by, we shall meet on that beautiful shore"; it means that you'll become "amazing grace" to the poor and to the forgotten crowds all around. I wonder if we really understood the resurrection, if any of us would ever come to church. No wonder the disciples were terrified.

I read the testimony of a young man, a freshman in college, who responded to Tony Campolo's invitation to do inner-city ministry in Philadelphia, Pennsylvania.[9] He said that in June he met a hundred other kids in a Baptist church in Philadelphia. Campolo preached for about an hour. When he finished, people were shouting, standing on the pews, clapping. "It was great," the young man said.

"Okay, gang, are you ready to go out there and tell 'em about Jesus?" Campolo asked. They all shouted, "Yea, let's go!"

They piled onto buses. They were singing and clapping, brimming with enthusiasm. As the bus drove deeper in the depths of the city, they gradually stopped singing, and all those college kids were just staring out the windows. "We were scared," he said.

"Then the bus pulled up in front of one of the worst-looking housing projects in Philadelphia. Campolo jumped on the bus, and said, 'Alright gang, get out there and tell 'em about Jesus. I'll be back at five o'clock.' "

They made their way off the bus and stood there on the

corner. They had prayer, then they spread out. The young man said, "I walked down the sidewalk and stopped before a huge tenement house. I gulped, said a prayer, and ventured inside. There was a terrible odor. Windows were out. No lights in the hall. I walked up one flight of stairs toward the door where I heard a baby crying. I knocked on the door."

"Who is it?" said a loud voice inside. Then the door cracked open and a woman, a woman holding a naked baby, peered out at me. "What you want?" she asked in a harsh, mean voice.

"I want to tell you about Jesus," he said.

With that, she swung the door open and began cursing him. She cursed him all the way down the hall, down the flight of steps, and out to the sidewalk. He felt terrible. "Look at me," he thought. "Some Christian I am. How in the world could somebody like me think that I could tell about Jesus?"

He sat down on the curb and cried. Then he looked up and noticed a store on the corner, windows all boarded up, bars over the door. He went to that store, walked in, looked around. Then he remembered—the baby had no diapers. The mother was smoking. "I bought a box of disposable diapers and a pack of cigarettes," he said.

"I walked back to the tenement house, said a prayer, walked in, walked up the flight of stairs, gulped, stood before the door, and knocked."

"Who is it?" said the voice inside. When she opened the door, he slid the box of diapers and those cigarettes in. She looked at them, looked at him and said, "Come in."

"I stepped into the dingy apartment," he recalled. "Sit down," she commanded. He sat down—on an old sofa—and began to play with the baby. "I put a diaper on the baby, even though I have never put one on before. When the woman offered me a cigarette, even though I don't smoke, I smoked. I stayed there all afternoon, talking, playing with the baby, listening to the woman.

"About four o'clock, the woman looked at me and said, 'Let me ask you something. What's a nice college boy like you doing in a place like this?' "

He said, "So I told her everything I knew about Jesus. It took me about five minutes." Then she said, "Pray for me and my baby that we can make it out of here alive." And he prayed.

That evening, after they were all back on the bus, Tony asked, "Well, gang, did any of you get to tell 'em about Jesus?" The young man said, "I not only got to tell 'em about Jesus, I met Jesus. I went to save somebody, and I ended up getting saved. I became a disciple."

That's just what might happen to any of us on any Sunday morning. Christ's resurrection is saturated with problems and surrounded with risk and is perhaps the most frightening good news you will ever hear. The gospel of Jesus Christ is danger-ous, messy, risky business because it liberates, it transforms, it offers freedom. It's terrifying. It demands faith—to act on that which is not and never will be completely understood.

It's Easter Sunday. Not only is the tomb empty, He is risen! Isn't that a sobering thought?

Evaluation of the Sermons

How do these sermons model evangelistic preaching that con-nects? The two sermons from the Old Testament focus on God's sovereignty in light of prevailing religious and cultural understandings. As shaped in Jesus' preaching, the *euangelion* challenges the status quo and offers a new way of looking at established practices, whether they be religious or cultural.

William Willimon, through his subtle use of humor, indicts certain forms of church worship for catering to the whims of the pew while neglecting the desires of God. "What does God like about worship?" Willimon queries. "What does God expect from Sunday morning?" He accuses churches of wanting "man-agers of consensus" instead of prophets. The sermon reminds hearers that God's desire for worship is to see "justice roll down like waters, and righteousness like an ever-flowing stream."

Many unchurched persons remain that way because they view the church as self-serving and hypocritical. Willimon's sermon harmonizes with some of their criticisms; he creates identification with their concerns about church. Though the sermon does not minimize the demands of the gospel, it could elicit a positive response from the unchurched because it voices their dismay. For the churched, any sermon that so faithfully heralds God's rightful place in worship should be heard as good news. One goal of evangelistic preaching is to remind a church of the distance between their profession and their practice.

With my Old Testament sermon, I attempt to remind the congregation of God's sovereignty at a time when many question the ability of the church to offer any viable response to a postmodern world. In the face of relativism, political correctness, religious fanaticism, the church often wrings its hands in fear. The sermon heralds the words of the prophet: " 'Don't be afraid of Assyria,' said Isaiah, 'God is in control.' " That message reflects the heart of the sermon and, as I understand it, the essence of the gospel. The church does not have to accommodate culture in order to be a viable conversation partner with culture. The church can be the church without looking like a movie theater and sounding like a rock concert. The church as "the language school for the kingdom of God" prepares God's people to share the good news. Any sermon that reminds believers of their vital role to speak on God's behalf is evangelistic.

The two New Testament sermons hold out the possibility of living the kingdom life, experiencing the gospel's liberation and freedom, while at the same time reminding their hearers of the intrinsic worth persons have in God's eyes. Raymond Bailey's sermon "You Can Go Home Again" exemplifies these evangelistic claims.

The sermon focuses on the young man's (often called the prodigal) search for real meaning in life. What he ultimately discovers is the gospel's way of making meaning, a new and different worldview from which he was accustomed. He also discovers the freedom he had to choose or reject such life. The gospel's message appears so couched in freedom that it never imposes its offer to new living on anyone. God gives human beings the freedom to choose or reject the gospel's offer of wholeness and salvation.

The young man in the story realizes that he is his father's child. One hallmark of the gospel is the claim that people have worth because they have been created in God's image and likeness, because God loves them and because Jesus Christ died for them. It's this gospel that invites church people to go home again. It's also wonderful news for those unchurched persons visiting in the service who may begin to realize that the home is theirs too.

My goal for the other New Testament evangelistic sermon was to exemplify the intrusiveness of the gospel. Most congregations know what to expect from an Easter sermon. Many unchurched persons who seldom grace church doors often find themselves in church on Easter Sunday. Their expectations may not be that much different from church folk on Easter Sunday. The preacher will highlight the resurrection story and discuss the joy and hope the resurrection holds for people. Such a message certainly embraces an aspect of Easter. However, the Lukan text lends itself to further reflection on the first Easter, especially if one presumes, as do most New Testament scholars, that verse 12 of Luke 24 is a later addition to the story. The first eleven verses leave us in a bit of a quandary because there appears to be more anxiety provoked by the women's report than joy and hope.

My aim in the sermon was to help the congregants move beyond a stereotypical understanding of the resurrection in order that they might be confronted with a different view of the gospel. I hoped to debunk a status quo interpretation of the text by showing that the disciples' reaction to Jesus' resurrection might have caused them to think differently about life. Evangelistic preaching should challenge hearers to recognize the gospel's new way of making meaning. The good news of the resurrection is not only the joy and hope given to the believing community, but it is a call of service to bring the good news to others. The empty tomb demands more than intellectual assent. An ethic of acting in the world on behalf of Christ remains the gospel's ultimate goal.

A unique Christian element found in the sermons is their inherent understanding that God continues to work in the world in and through the church. No news is any better than that God is still reconciling the world to himself in Christ. As Christ's living presence is made real through worship and service, the church brings the gospel to the world. All the sermons call for transformation; a conversion of attitudes and actions as a result of hearing good news is their goal. The sermons present the gospel as a new way of looking at life.

Another element of the gospel is invitation. Each sermon communicates an invitational tone: from a call to authentic worship, to recognizing God's sovereignty, to an invitation to come home to faith, to a call to serve Christ in the world, the sermons invite people into the gospel's world, the kingdom of God. Such is the ambition of evangelistic preaching.

The sermons generally follow the inductive model we discussed in chapter three. That is, they do not presume complete adherence to a set proposition before unfolding the heart of their messages. The sermons invite the hearers to active participation in discovering their evangelistic message.

Questions for Reflection

The following questions provide a framework for evaluating

and composing evangelistic sermons. The questions are representative, so please add to the list generously, making sure your concerns are addressed.

1. What is uniquely Christian about the sermon?

2. What is the sermon's gospel message?

3. Are issues of *euangelion* clearly distinguished? (For example, the worth of persons, liberation, freedom, forgiveness of sin, living a kingdom life, the intrusiveness of the gospel and so on.)

4. Does the sermon offer a new way of looking at life, a new way of making meaning? If so, how?

5. Does the sermon offer a viable theological challenge of the status quo? If so, how?

6. Does the sermon speak good news to believers and unbelievers?

7. Is the sermon faithful to the biblical text? On what do you base your judgment?

8. Does the sermon follow a deductive or inductive movement? On what do you base your judgment?

9. How does the sermon balance the nowness and futureness of the gospel?

10. Does the sermon maintain an invitational tone?

7/Responding to the Gospel: Now What Will You Do?

*Y*ou've finished preaching an evangelistic sermon. What happens next? Do you end the liturgy with a benediction and send the masses back to their workaday worlds? Do you shift into the weeping-evangelist mode, begging everyone to "accept Jesus" and hoping that someone, anyone, "walks the aisle"? Or do you allow the congregation, corporately and individually, freedom to respond to the gospel in their own way? Well, it depends on whom you ask.

My denominational identity colors my perspective on the subject. Southern Baptist churches close worship services with an explicit time of invitation. In other words, Southern Baptists expect the preacher to *invite* persons to respond intentionally and visibly to the sermon they've just heard. Whether at an evangelistic service, a service celebrating baptism or the Lord's Supper, or a traditional worship service, congregations expect an invitation. As a rule Baptists, claiming the free church tradition, pride themselves on being nonliturgical. That may be true by definition, but in practice "the invitation" constitutes part of the liturgy almost universally among Southern Baptists.

At the end of a sermon, before the benediction, Baptists expect and feel comfortable with a call to respond to the gospel: an invitation.

Isn't that what usually happens when an evangelist finishes a sermon? Everyone is familiar with the Billy Graham Crusades. He always closes the service with an invitation. Graham asks people who are making a decision for Christ to leave their seats and gather in front of the platform area, where trained counselors talk with them and give them some important literature. Isn't that the way evangelistic services always end, even in church?

I discussed the subject with a colleague who has experience with a wide spectrum of evangelical churches, and he told me that closing a service with an invitation was the exception rather than the rule. According to him, most evangelical churches would be as uncomfortable as mainline denominational churches with the preacher asking people to leave their pews and walk down the aisle to accept or to rededicate their lives to Christ. They would view such a practice as manipulative or coercive, relying on the preacher's understanding of coming to faith as normative for all Christians. My friend's observations surprised me. Isn't it funny how we assume that everyone does things the way we do them?

So far, then, we have two specific answers to our question of what happens next: after every sermon comes an invitation; or an invitation is a presumptuous device used by pushy preachers, so we don't do that here. That leaves me in a quandary.

Though I'm a Southern Baptist, I don't think every service should end with an invitation. One would think that such a confession, obviously bordering on heresy, would make me anathema within my denominational family. It probably will, but I have a kind of proof text or two for my position. John A. Broadus, a predecessor who taught preaching at the Southern

Baptist Theological Seminary and defined preaching for years among Southern Baptists, advised that not every sermon should end with an invitation. Charles Haddon Spurgeon did not like the regular use of invitations either. I agree with them.

On the other hand, the gospel, in its essence, is invitational. It calls people to respond; it invites allegiance to its claims. The apostle Peter understood this affirmation when he said, "Repent and be baptized every one of you in the name of Jesus Christ" (Acts 2:38). The gospel beckons and entices people into its world. Invitation models its call. So it seems that somewhere in our ecclesiology there should be a place for an invitation to occur. I think worship may be the spot; the location from which we proclaim the gospel of God and of his Christ seems naturally invitational. Help the congregation know that the gospel demands some response. The biblical witness clearly indicates that an invitation to respond grows naturally out of the proclamation of the gospel.

In other words, the dilemma *appears* to hinge on whether to invite or not to invite following a sermon. My interpretation sees the problem based more on methodological disagreements than on the idea of allowing the gospel to summon response. The issue, as I see it, is not *whether* to invite but *how* to offer a responsible invitation that does justice to the gospel.

I offer the following musings (and they are just that, rather than procedures) for several reasons. Tampering with the liturgical rituals of a church is akin to juggling nitroglycerin. You know there's going to be an explosion—you're just not sure when. Prescribing a change in the worship order, advising the abandonment of a well-worn ritual or challenging the statement "We've never done it that way before" connotes *tampering*. Listening to musings is much safer; you can take them or leave them. Second, my literary research found little written on the subject of evangelistic invitations. What I found was monotonously predictable, enough only to muse over. Finally, based on fervent discussions that took place the last time I taught the course "Evangelistic Preaching," I have come to the conclusion that being too dogmatic about evangelistic invitations yields more heat than light. It's more acceptable to muse than to pontificate. So let's muse together.

Avoid the Term *Invitation*

For you invitational types, don't get too upset. Remember, we're only musing! If the very nature of the gospel is invitational, why would we want to avoid the term *invitation*? For the same reason that, for example, I try to avoid the term *inerrant* to describe the Scriptures. In my context, *inerrancy* has been used as a shibboleth to define political allegiances within a denominational feud. Its referent, the complete veracity of the Bible, became mired in driving factional machinations. As a preacher, I am aware of the power of words and how they can be used and misused, understood and misunderstood. Do you remember the childhood ditty most of us memorized almost from birth: "Sticks and stones can break my bones, but words can never hurt me"? Have you ever heard anything more twisted? We've all been hurt by words spoken in anger or hurt. Words can cut with the precision and depth of a two-edged sword. When words become charged with meanings far beyond their dictionary sense, we must use them with great care. Otherwise we risk miscommunication.

The word *invitation* carries much ecclesiastical baggage. It often communicates manipulative tent revivals complete with an evangelist working the crowd into a frenzy. Jonas Nightingale, the character played by Steve Martin in the film *Leap of Faith,* mastered the stereotypical emotional invitation. Such negative images fuel the demise of the term. For others, the word *invitation* falls outside their liturgical framework in the same way that recitation of the Apostles' Creed falls outside the realm of most evangelicals. An invitation becomes "what those other Christians do when they finish a service."

We don't want the name we give to a liturgical element to keep someone from responding to the gospel. I'm willing to give up the word *invitation* to communicate the idea. But I'm not willing to drop the concept of calling people to respond to the gospel's message.

If you drop the word *invitation* from your liturgical vocabulary, what do you use to define the place that used to be known by that word? How about "Responding to the Gospel," "Response to the Word," "Hymn of Response" or "Answering the Gospel's Call"? With a little imagination, we can muster many terms that offer the gospel without the baggage associated with that word *invitation.*

Expanding the Options for Response

I have made the point numerous times that the gospel is for unbelievers and believers too. This being the case, offer a response that *includes* rather than excludes. In other words, don't just invite people to walk the aisle. There's nothing magical, or spiritual for that matter, about aisle walking. At this point someone will be tempted to quote the proof text for such practice: "Everyone therefore who acknowledges me before others . . ." (Mt 10:32). This mindset assumes that coming forward in church is the only way for people to acknowledge Christ before others—a rather myopic understanding of faith, to say the least. For some people the visible and physical movement from the pew to the front of the sanctuary symbolizes the commitment they have made to Christ; it embodies the response they are making to what they have heard. For others, however, the prospect of being vulnerable in front of a group of strangers may actually prevent them from coming to Christ. Christian discipleship endures as a process in which no single, normative formula makes that happen. The book of Acts shows a variety of ways people responded to the gospel—all authentic. Broaden your options and allow the Spirit to blow as God chooses.

So how can we expand the options? First, make sure your request grows naturally out of the sermon the congregation just heard. If you preached about receiving forgiveness, you should invite the congregation to receive forgiveness. If the sermon focused on the good news of God's people responding to the needs of hungry persons, you should invite them to feed someone who is hungry. Think about immediate responses, as well as those that your hearers can put into practice when they go to work Monday morning, when they face classmates in school, when they bump into friends at the grocery store. The gospel is about life. Offer your hearers a chance to respond throughout their daily experiences, not just a fleeting chance to walk the aisle. And remember, the response you might make is not the normative one. Keep the options of possible responses open; the gospel ranges wider than typical evangelistic invitations allow.

Second, offer a response to seekers that honors their desire for anonymity. The church could provide cards in the pew racks that seekers could fill out, asking for a time to visit with the pastor, other staff members or committed laypersons. The card could provide a place for a person to ask a question; the question could be answered by mail or via a telephone call. The person making the query would choose the option. This non-threatening invitation would allow seekers to respond at their own time, in their own way and according to their own pace. They would be free to deal with *their* questions and not feel that they were being corralled into a one-size-fits-all faith. As with those who reacted to the apostle Paul in Acts 17, if people leave worship thinking to themselves, *I'll hear more about this,* then the gospel is being planted.

Another option would be to let people know that the ministerial staff and some church members will be available after the service for brief, informal chats. This again would allow people to meet Christians informally and, most important, in a non-threatening way. I served Hurstbourne Baptist Church in Louisville, Kentucky, for nearly two years as their interim pastor. During that time we began an informal reception for visitors and guests following the Sunday-morning worship service. Several people set up a table with some light refreshments in the fellowship hall. The hall was easily accessible, and church members provided assistance directing guests to it. I, the staff, our spouses and many laypersons met with visitors following the service. A guest register was made available. We worked hard to make sure people felt no obligation or compulsion to do anything at these receptions. They were as they were billed, an informal time to get to know people. Because of the receptions, I was personally able to make follow-up visits with some seekers and to share the gospel with them at a point when they were willing and anxious to hear the good news.

Christian discipleship is a matter of mentoring and bringing people into the faith through relationships. As people hear the gospel preached, our hope is that it will move them to make an appropriate response. The church must be ready to support them when they do.

Third, why not allow baptism to be the place of public profession of faith in Christ? Many people have walked an aisle and said to an evangelist that they wanted to "accept Christ into their heart," yet had little understanding about what they were doing. I am not questioning the evangelist's motives in inviting them to come or their motives of responding to the invitation. Nor do I doubt the validity of their claim that they have made a decision to follow Christ. That decision, nevertheless, needs nurturing. The parable of the sower (Mk 4:3-9) looms ominously. Too often we assume that the "profession of faith" following an evangelistic sermon is a mature statement of belief when, in fact, the seed has just landed on fertile soil.

Most seeker-targeted churches, by necessity, have developed

excellent ways to nurture people in the faith once they have made an initial decision to pursue discipleship. Personal mentoring, discipleship groups and seeker-sensitive seminars provide firm footing on difficult terrain. Without such discipleship, the results can be painfully sad. I know of a church that had sixty-three "decisions for Christ" as a result of an evangelistic crusade. One year following the crusade, none—not one of those sixty-three—had become an active disciple. Evangelism had won the harvest yet lost the crop.

Baptism is rightly the place for a public confession of one's faith. Following a time of nurturing and cultivation, new believers can articulate a sound understanding of their faith in Christ, one that has taken root. The confession of faith at baptism might involve candidates' sharing their personal testimony about their decision to become a Christian. They could describe how their lives had been touched and transformed by the good news (1 Jn 1:1-4). Another approach could be incorporated into the baptismal ceremony. The officiant could ask pointed questions about the candidate's faith: Do you believe that Jesus Christ is the Son of God who came to seek and to save persons from their sin? Do you believe that Jesus Christ died for the sins of the world? Do you believe that you are a sinner for whom Christ died? Do you believe that Jesus Christ was raised from the dead and now reigns eternally with God the Father and the Holy Spirit? Following the questions or the testimony, the candidate's baptism becomes a direct symbol and a part of his or her professed faith. Baptism becomes testimonial, an acted-out sermon. Of course, Christian discipleship and cultivation must continue as a process throughout life.

Expanding the options for response includes being innovative in ways you invite people to accept the gospel. Some preachers follow a rote formula when making evangelistic appeals: "Perhaps you are here this morning, and you need to accept Jesus Christ as your personal Savior. Perhaps you need to rededicate your life to Christ. Maybe you have decided to make this place your church home. Whatever your decision, Christ is here to receive you." After hearing these words several times at the end of a sermon, most people tend to respond by thinking, *Well, the service is over.* Ronald W. Johnson, director of evangelism for the Georgia Baptist Convention, has suggested a possible alternative—what he calls an inductive invitation.[1] Johnson has tried this approach. When he finished a sermon, he asked the congregation to pray. He then led them in a focused prayer of thanks to God, instead of offering them something he felt they needed. The following is the prayer he used:[2]

> This morning, take a few moments to thank God for your salvation. Remember that time when you asked Jesus Christ to be your personal Savior. A time when you repented of your sins and asked Christ to forgive you of all your wrongs. A time when you told Him that you were ready to let Him be Lord in your life. And a time when you followed Jesus in believer's baptism. Remember, and thank Him.

In the next part of the prayer, Johnson led them to remember the person who shared Christ with them, to thank God for the first church they joined and to remember and thank God for the times they ministered and witnessed to others. Johnson continued:

> Now, for some of you here this morning, you know that you cannot pray a prayer of thanks to God. You have searched your mind and you cannot remember a time when you personally asked Jesus to become Lord of your life. Or you cannot remember when or if you moved your church membership from your home church to this city where you now live. Perhaps there are others here who cannot remember ever telling anyone about Jesus or ministering to another in some way.
>
> Lord, help us to think on these things. And help us to

decide what our needs are and in what way we need to respond to what you are telling us as we think together this morning. We ask you to help us remember and help us to respond to your calling, in Jesus' name. Amen.

Johnson shows how an evangelistic invitation can take on new meaning by moving away from an "if you need" appeal to a "thank God when you remember" appeal. He says, "When we remember events in our lives, those things we have omitted or overlooked can surface and convict us quickly."

If you try an invitation like this one, be sure that it has some connection to the sermon you preached. No matter the type of appeal, it must grow naturally from the sermon the congregation has heard.

Some pastors ask people to make a personal commitment where they sit, registering that commitment on a card. Others provide an information packet that visitors can pick up at the close of a service. The packet includes material describing how a person can respond to the gospel. Some seeker-targeted churches maintain an information table, easily accessible and nonthreatening. Persons can choose from a variety of discipleship materials appropriately chosen for seekers. Some churches provide information printed in their Sunday-morning bulletin describing the response portion of the service and offering several suggestions about ways people can respond.

Remember, some people have no idea what is taking place in church. As you expand the options, keep these people in mind. Allow the congregation, corporately and individually, freedom to respond to the gospel in their own way. Give freedom to the Holy Spirit's unction. The sky's the limit for innovative ways to call persons to respond to what they have experienced in worship.

Preparing the Call for Response

Like the sermon, the call to commitment should be thought out and planned in advance. Think about what you will say when you finish the sermon. Decide whether the sermon will end with a closing prayer, followed by the time for response, or whether you will move naturally from the last section of the sermon into the response time. Raymond Bailey suggests that the appeal really begins with the introduction of the sermon; to him, the entire sermon forms an invitation to faith. When he invites a response, it unfolds well planned and blended into the fabric of the sermon. Planning prevents this time from becoming routine and meaningless. Of course, allow for the Spirit to lead. But the Spirit's leading may be best manifested through prayerful preparation.

Be *specifically general* with the appeal. Oxymorons often describe Christian faith. You want to be specific so that people know what ballpark you're in but general enough to include their circumstances. Be specific enough to give them examples of what they can do, general enough to allow them imaginative freedom for a response appropriate to their needs. Too specific and you exclude everyone; too general and you include all, so you have included none.

Some people, especially seekers, view what happens in church as strangely ritualistic and experientially irrelevant. Guide your hearers through the invitational time directly and clearly. Help them know that the gospel includes them. The inclusive call of the gospel has already been demonstrated in the sermon. Now provide clues so different hearers can embody what they have heard.

The last time Tony Campolo preached at Southern Seminary, he closed the sermon with a request. He asked students and faculty to consider coming to Philadelphia to work with him and his staff doing inner-city ministry there. He asked people to put their name on a piece of paper if they would be willing to help the ministry in some way. He closed with prayer. After the service he met with many people, collected names and described the many ways people could serve in Philadelphia. He was specifically general, and many responded. People heard the gospel that day and became doers of what they heard.

Avoid buzzwords, clichés and religious jargon at this time. I have emphasized these issues in my discussions of evangelism and preaching in general. But during the appeal it is essential that you purge your vocabulary of the rote shibboleths that so easily creep in. Inviting people to active participation in kingdom life takes sincerity, passion and empathy. Warm authenticity invites genuine response. Listen to tapes of your worship services and evaluate the language you use. You'll be surprised by what you hear.

Make sure that you save time to call for response. Too often people think that when the sermon ends, so does the service. If you have backed your listeners up to their lunchtime, natural phenomena of hunger may cry more loudly than your words. Help your worship leadership team (hopefully in concert with the church's worship committee) view the time as integral to worship and not an orphaned appendage. Try different approaches. Perhaps "bookending" the appeal would be a way to ensure adequate time. Begin the worship service with your invitation—a preview of what will come. Then end the service by concluding your suggestions for response. The elements of worship that come between the bookends enhance and reinforce the gospel's call.

Avoid sensationalism, emotionalism or manipulation. The concern for success becomes an evil tempter during this time in a service. Measure success by your faithful proclamation of the gospel, not by how many people come forward after your call. You always want to keep the best interests of your hearers at the forefront. The gospel demands no less. The sermon you preached provides the basis for the call. The time to invite is just that—a time to invite. It's not time to repreach the sermon or to add a "dying dog story" as the grand finale to what has come before. Here is the place where you give people time to react to the gospel they have heard. If you have preached the gospel clearly, inviting response will flow naturally and freely.

The worship service is nearly over. The prayers have been prayed, the hymns sung, the confessions spoken, the affirmations voiced, the offering collected, and you have preached. The gospel has been proclaimed. It says to you and to every person who has heard, "Now what will you do?"

Summing Up

My sincere hope is that these musings, and, indeed, the entire book, have helped you rethink evangelistic sermons. The gospel hovers over the church, waiting for us to proclaim its transforming power into the world. In our present context the gospel may be a stumbling block to some and foolishness to others, but to those who are called it is "Christ the power of God and the wisdom of God" (1 Cor 1:24). "For 'Everyone who calls on the name of the Lord shall be saved.' But how are they to call on one in whom they have not believed? And how are they to believe in one of whom they have never heard? And how are they to hear without someone to proclaim him?" (Rom 10:13-14).

How will they hear without someone to proclaim? That's our calling. Preach good news.

Notes

Chapter 1: How Are They to Hear?

[1] This chapter is adapted from my article "How Are They to Hear? Evangelism and Proclamation," *Review and Expositor* 90 (1993): 101-13. Used by permission.

[2] William F. Graham, "Billy Graham on What He Does Best: Insights for Fellow Evangelists," *Christianity Today* 27 (September 2, 1983): 31.

[3] For a developed explanation of the incarnational model for preaching, see chapter 3 in my *Preaching Sermons That Connect: Effective Communication Through Identification* (Downers Grove, Ill.: InterVarsity Press, 1992).

[4] Phillips Brooks, *Lectures on Preaching* (New York: Dutton, 1877), p. 8.

[5] See "God the Holy Spirit," article II.C of *The Baptist Faith and Message* (Nashville: Sunday School Board of the Southern Baptist Convention, 1963).

[6] I have dealt with some of these issues as they relate to preaching in "Back to the Future: Preaching into the Third Millennium," *Preaching* 7 (1992): 27-31.

[7] Donald C. Posterski, *Reinventing Evangelism: New Strategies for Presenting Christ in Today's World* (Downers Grove, Ill.: InterVarsity Press, 1989), p. 11.

[8] Bill Leonard, *Word of God Across the Ages* (Nashville: Broadman, 1981), pp. 77-87.

[9] Posterski, *Reinventing Evangelism*, p. 65.

[10]Alfred Krass, "Bulldozer Strategies? Preach to Convince, Not to Condemn," *The Other Side* 21 (1985): 62.

[11]Richard Armstrong, *The Pastor-Evangelist in the Parish* (Louisville, Ky.: Westminster/John Knox Press, 1990), p. 17.

[12]Martin E. Marty, "The Water's Fine," *The Christian Century*, July 1-8, 1992, p. 663.

[13]Two of Barna's earlier books include *The Frog in the Kettle* (Ventura, Calif.: Regal, 1990) and *User Friendly Churches* (Ventura, Calif.: Regal, 1991).

[14]Posterski, *Reinventing Evangelism*, p. 143.

[15]K. Anderson, *Persuasion Theory and Practice* (Boston: Allyn & Bacon, 1971), p. 6.

[16]T. Scheidel, *Persuasive Speaking* (Glenview, Ill.: Scott Foresman, 1967), p. 1.

[17]Robert Bostrom, *Persuasion* (Englewood Cliffs, N.J.: Prentice-Hall, 1983), p. 11. For further discussions of persuasion as it relates to evangelistic preaching, see Ronald Sleeth, *Persuasive Preaching* (New York: Harper & Brothers, 1956); Alan Walker, *Evangelistic Preaching* (Grand Rapids, Mich.: Zondervan, 1988); and A. Duane Litfin, "The Perils of Persuasive Preaching," *Christianity Today*, February 4, 1977, pp. 14-17.

[18]Lewis A. Drummond, *Leading Your Church in Evangelism* (Nashville: Broadman, 1975), p. 36.

[19]For further reading on the subject of ethics and persuasion, see Raymond W. McLaughlin, *The Ethics of Persuasive Preaching* (Grand Rapids, Mich.: Baker Book House, 1979); B. J. Diggs, "Persuasion and Ethics," *Quarterly Journal of Speech* 73 (1964): 359-73.

[20]Ralph L. Lewis, *Persuasive Preaching Today* (Wilmore, Ky.: Asbury Theological Seminary, 1982), p. 112.

[21]Ibid., p. 132.

Chapter 2: Who's Afraid of the Big Bad Wolf?

[1]Vernon L. Stanfield, *Effective Evangelistic Preaching* (Grand Rapids, Mich.: Baker Book House, 1965), p. 15.

[2]Alan Walker, *Evangelistic Preaching* (Grand Rapids, Mich.: Zondervan, 1988), p. 72.

[3]C. H. Dodd, *The Apostolic Preaching and Its Developments* (1936; rpt.

Grand Rapids, Mich.: Baker Book House, 1980).

[4]For a detailed critique of Dodd's dichotomy of *kērygma and didachē,* see Robert H. Mounce, *The Essential Nature of New Testament Preaching* (Grand Rapids, Mich.: Eerdmans, 1960).

[5]Dodd, *Apostolic Preaching,* p. 17.

[6]Ibid., pp. 21-23.

[7]Stanfield, *Effective Evangelistic Preaching,* p. 11.

[8]Robert Menzies, *Preaching and Pastoral Evangelism* (Edinburgh: Saint Andrew Press, 1962), p. 15.

[9]Michael Green, *Evangelism Through the Local Church: A Comprehensive Guide to All Aspects of Evangelism* (Nashville: Oliver-Nelson, 1992), p. 7.

[10]William H. Willimon, *The Intrusive Word: Preaching to the Unbaptized* (Grand Rapids, Mich.: Eerdmans, 1994), p. 16.

[11]Ibid., p. 39.

[12]Walter Brueggemann, *Biblical Perspectives on Evangelism: Living in a Three-Storied Universe* (Nashville: Abingdon, 1993), p. 34.

[13]J. B. Philips, *Your God Is Too Small* (New York: Macmillan, 1961).

[14]Brueggemann, *Biblical Perspectives on Evangelism,* p. 35.

[15]Ibid., p. 129.

[16]Dodd, *Apostolic Preaching,* p. 33.

[17]Richard Stoll Armstrong, *The Pastor-Evangelist in the Parish* (Louisville, Ky.: Westminster/John Knox Press, 1990), p. 13.

[18]Thomas G. Long made these remarks during the E. Y. Mullins Lectures on Preaching at Southern Baptist Theological Seminary, Louisville, Kentucky, March 1990.

Chapter 3: It Sure Doesn't Look Like an Evangelistic Sermon

[1]C. E. Autrey, *Evangelistic Sermons* (Grand Rapids, Mich.: Zondervan, 1962); John R. Bisagno, *The Power of Positive Preaching to the Lost* (Nashville: Broadman, 1972); Andrew W. Blackwood, ed., *Evangelical Sermons of Our Day* (New York: Harper & Brothers, 1959); Clovis G. Chappell, *Evangelistic Sermons of Clovis G. Chappell* (Nashville: Abingdon, 1973); Ellis A. Fuller, *Evangelistic Sermons* (Nashville: Broadman, 1953); G. B. Vick, *Soul-Winning Sermons* (Grand Rapids, Mich.: Zondervan, 1958); Charles L. Wallis, ed., *88 Evangelistic Sermons* (New York: Harper & Row, 1964).

²Autrey, *Evangelistic Sermons*, pp. 13-25.

³Alan Walker, "Religion or Christ," in *Evangelical Sermons of Our Day*, ed. Andrew W. Blackwood (New York: Harper & Brothers, 1959), pp. 137-47.

⁴See Thomas G. Long, *Preaching and the Literary Forms of the Bible* (Philadelphia: Fortress, 1989).

⁵Two well-known monographs are Fred Craddock's *As One Without Authority* (Nashville: Abingdon, 1971) and Ralph Lewis's *Inductive Preaching* (Westchester, Ill.: Crossway, 1983).

⁶Chappell, *Evangelistic Sermons*, p. 14.

⁷Raymond Bailey and James Blevins, *Dramatic Monologues: Making the Bible Live* (Nashville: Broadman, 1990).

Chapter 4: Preaching Good News from the Old Testament

¹I am presuming the Old and New Testament canon as presented in the Protestant Bible.

²Elizabeth Achtemeier, *Preaching from the Old Testament* (Louisville, Ky.: Westminster/John Knox Press, 1989), p. 21. See particularly her chapter "Why the Old Testament Is Necessary for the Church."

³Ibid.

⁴Faris Daniel Whitesell, *Evangelistic Preaching and the Old Testament* (Chicago: Moody Bible Institute, 1947), p. 7.

⁵Ibid., p. 18.

⁶Craig L. Blomberg, "Form Criticism," in *Dictionary of Jesus and the Gospels*, ed. Joel B. Green, Scot McKnight and I. Howard Marshall (Downers Grove, Ill.: InterVarsity Press, 1992), pp. 243-50.

⁷C. H. Dodd, *The Apostolic Preaching and Its Developments* (1936; rpt. Grand Rapids, Mich.: Baker Book House, 1980), p. 33.

Chapter 5: Preaching Good News from the New Testament

¹James L. Blevins, *Revelation*, Knox Preaching Guides (Atlanta: John Knox Press, 1984), p. 2. Another helpful book for preachers is James L. Blevins, *Revelation as Drama* (Nashville: Broadman, 1984).

²Thomas G. Long, "Preaching Apocalyptic Literature," *Review and Expositor* 90 (Summer 1993): 373.

³Ibid., p. 379.

⁴Ibid.

Chapter 6: Practice What You Preach

[1]This sermon is published in William H. Willimon and Stanley Hauerwas, *Preaching to Strangers: Evangelism in Today's World* (Louisville, Ky.: Westminster/John Knox Press, 1992), pp. 91-97. Used by permission. The author quotes Scripture from the Revised Standard Version and his own paraphrase.

[2]Scripture quotations in this sermon are the author's paraphrase, based on the New Revised Standard Version.

[3]Tex Sample, *U.S. Lifestyles and Mainline Churches: A Key to Reaching People in the 90's* (Louisville, Ky.: Westminster/John Knox Press, 1990).

[4]Walter Brueggemann, *Interpretation and Obedience: From Faithful Reading to Faithful Living* (Minneapolis: Fortress, 1991), pp. 41-69.

[5]Sample, *U.S. Lifestyles and Mainline Churches,* pp. 42-43.

[6]Kenneth Myers, *All God's Children and Blue Suede Shoes: Christians and Popular Culture* (Wheaton, Ill.: Crossway, 1989), pp. 18-19.

[7]George Barna, *The Frog in the Kettle* (Ventura, Calif.: Regal, 1990), and *User Friendly Churches* (Ventura, Calif.: Regal, 1991).

[8]Scripture quotations in this sermon are the author's paraphrase, based on the New Revised Standard Version.

[9]This story appears in William H. Willimon, *The Intrusive Word: Preaching to the Unbaptized* (Grand Rapids, Mich.: Eerdmans, 1994), pp. 74-77. Used by permission.

Chapter 7: Responding to the Gospel

[1]Ronald W. Johnson, "Thank You, Lord: An Inductive Approach to the Invitation," *Preaching,* November-December 1993, pp. 27-29.

[2]Ibid.

For Further Reading

Books

Abraham, William J. *The Logic of Evangelism*. Grand Rapids, Mich.: Eerdmans, 1989.

Achtemeier, Elizabeth. *Preaching from the Old Testament*. Louisville, Ky.: Westminster/John Knox Press, 1989.

Anderson, K. *Persuasion Theory and Practice*. Boston: Allyn & Bacon, 1971.

Armstrong, Richard S. *The Pastor-Evangelist in the Parish*. Louisville, Ky.: Westminster/John Knox Press, 1990.

_____. *The Pastor-Evangelist in Worship*. Philadelphia: Westminster Press, 1986.

Autrey, C. E. *Evangelistic Sermons*. Grand Rapids, Mich.: Zondervan, 1962.

Bailey, Raymond, and James Blevins. *Dramatic Monologues: Making the Bible Live*. Nashville: Broadman, 1990.

Barna, George. *The Frog in the Kettle*. Ventura, Calif.: Regal, 1990.

_____. *User Friendly Churches*. Ventura, Calif.: Regal, 1991.

Bisagno, John R. *The Power of Positive Preaching to the Lost*. Nashville: Broadman, 1972.

Blackwood, Andrew W., ed. *Evangelical Sermons of Our Day*. New York: Harper & Brothers, 1959.

Blevins, James L. *Revelation*. Knox Preaching Guides. Atlanta: John Knox Press, 1984.

_____. *Revelation as Drama.* Nashville: Broadman, 1984.

Bostrom, Robert. *Persuasion.* Englewood Cliffs, N.J.: Prentice-Hall, 1983.

Brueggemann, Walter. *Biblical Perspectives on Evangelism: Living in a Three-Storied Universe.* Nashville: Abingdon, 1993.

Chappell, Clovis G. *Evangelistic Sermons of Clovis G. Chappell.* Nashville: Abingdon, 1973.

Conn, Harvie M. *Evangelism: Doing Justice and Preaching Grace.* Grand Rapids, Mich.: Zondervan, 1982.

Craddock, Fred. *As One Without Authority.* Nashville: Abingdon, 1971.

Davis, Ozora S. *Evangelistic Preaching.* New York: Revell, 1921.

Dodd, C. H. *The Apostolic Preaching and Its Developments.* 1936; rpt. Grand Rapids, Mich.: Baker Book House, 1980.

Douglas, J. D., ed. *The Work of an Evangelist.* Minneapolis: World Wide Publications, 1984.

Drummond, Lewis. *Leading Your Church in Evangelism.* Nashville: Broadman, 1975.

Engel, James F. *Contemporary Christian Communication, Its Theory and Practice.* Nashville: Nelson, 1979.

Fuller, Ellis A. *Evangelistic Sermons.* Nashville: Broadman, 1953.

Graham, Robert G. *Dynamics of Evangelistic Preaching: Preaching the Word with Power.* Cleveland, Tenn.: Pathway, 1989.

Green, Michael. *Evangelism Through the Local Church: A Comprehensive Guide to All Aspects of Evangelism.* Nashville: Oliver-Nelson, 1992.

Gresham, Charles, and Keith Keeran. *Evangelistic Preaching.* Joplin, Mo.: College Press, 1991.

Harding, Joe A. *Have I Told You Lately? Preaching to Help People and Churches Grow.* Pasadena, Calif.: Church Growth, 1982.

Johannesen, Richard L. *Ethics and Persuasion.* New York: Random House, 1967.

Larson, David L. *The Evangelism Mandate: Recovering the Centrality of Gospel Preaching.* Wheaton, Ill.: Crossway, 1992.

Lewis, Ralph L. *Inductive Preaching.* Westchester, Ill.: Crossway, 1983.

_____. *Persuasive Preaching Today.* Wilmore, Ky.: Asbury Theological Seminary, 1982.

Lischer, Richard. *Speaking of Jesus: Finding the Words for Witness.* Philadelphia: Fortress, 1982.

Long, Thomas G. *Preaching and the Literary Forms of the Bible.* Philadelphia: Fortress, 1989.

Loscalzo, Craig A. *Preaching Sermons That Connect: Effective Communication Through Identification.* Downers Grove, Ill.: InterVarsity Press, 1992.

McLaughlin, Raymond W. *The Ethics of Persuasive Preaching.* Grand Rapids, Mich.: Baker Book House, 1979.

Menzies, Robert. *Preaching and Pastoral Evangelism.* Edinburgh: Saint Andrew Press, 1962.

Mounce, Robert H. *The Essential Nature of New Testament Preaching.* Grand Rapids, Mich.: Eerdmans, 1960.

Myers, Kenneth. *All God's Children and Blue Suede Shoes: Christians and Popular Culture.* Wheaton, Ill.: Crossway, 1989.

Perry, Lloyd Merle, and John R. Strubhar. *Evangelistic Preaching.* Chicago: Moody Press, 1979.

Posterski, Donald C. *Reinventing Evangelism: New Strategies for Presenting Christ in Today's World.* Downers Grove, Ill.: InterVarsity Press, 1989.

Sample, Tex. *U.S. Lifestyles and Mainline Churches: A Key to Reaching People in the 90's.* Louisville, Ky.: Westminster/John Knox Press, 1990.

Scheidel, T. *Persuasive Speaking.* Glenview, Ill.: Scott Foresman, 1967.

Sleeth, Ronald. *Persuasive Preaching.* New York: Harper & Brothers, 1956.

Stanfield, Vernon L. *Effective Evangelistic Preaching.* Grand Rapids, Mich.: Baker Book House, 1965.

Vick, G. B. *Soul-Winning Sermons.* Grand Rapids, Mich.: Zondervan, 1958.

Walker, Alan. *Evangelistic Preaching.* Grand Rapids, Mich.: Zondervan, 1988.

Wallis, Charles L., ed. *88 Evangelistic Sermons.* New York: Harper & Row, 1964.

Webster, Douglas D. *Selling Jesus: What's Wrong with Marketing the Church.* Downers Grove, Ill.: InterVarsity Press, 1992.

Whitesell, Faris Daniel. *Evangelistic Preaching and the Old Testament.* Chicago: Moody Bible Institute, 1947.

Willimon, William H., and Stanley Hauerwas. *The Intrusive Word:*

Preaching to the Unbaptized. Grand Rapids, Mich.: Eerdmans, 1994.

————. *Preaching to Strangers: Evangelism in Today's World.* Louisville, Ky.: Westminster/John Knox Press, 1992.

Wirt, Sherwood E., ed. *Evangelism: The Next Ten Years.* Waco, Tex.: Word, 1978.

Articles

Alexander, James. "Evangelism: Preaching and Pastoral." *Expository Times* 60 (July 1949): 286-89.

Augsburger, Myron S. "Rethinking the Evangelistic Sermon." *Leadership* 11 (Summer 1990): 62-64, 66-68.

Bailey, Raymond H. "Ethics in Preaching." *Review and Expositor* 86 (1989): 533-46.

Blomberg, Craig L. "Form Criticism." In *Dictionary of Jesus and the Gospels,* pp. 243-50. Edited by Joel B. Green, Scot McKnight and I. Howard Marshall. Downers Grove, Ill.: InterVarsity Press, 1992.

Brunsting, Bernard. "Evangelistic Preaching." *Christianity Today* 7 (November 9, 1962): 16-18.

Coleman, Robert E. "Evangelistic Preaching." *Fundamentalist Journal* 7 (February 1988): 46.

Diggs, B. J. "Persuasion and Ethics." *Quarterly Journal of Speech* 73 (1964): 359-73.

Dollar, Truman. "The Invitation: Is It Really Necessary?" *Fundamentalist Journal* 4 (April 1985): 66.

Graham, William F. "Billy Graham on What He Does Best: Insights for Fellow Evangelists." *Christianity Today* 27 (September 2, 1983): 28-31.

Henry, Jim. "Preparing the Evangelistic Message." *Preaching* 6 (March-April 1991): 16-18.

Johnson, Ron W. "Thank You, Lord: An Inductive Approach to the Invitation." *Preaching* 9 (November-December 1993): 27-29.

Keifert, Patrick. "Guess Who's Coming to Worship? Worship and Evangelism." *Word & World* 9 (1989): 46-51.

Krass, Alfred. "Bulldozer Strategies? Preach to Convince, Not to Condemn." *The Other Side* 21 (1985): 62-63.

Lawton, Kim A. "Is High-Tech Preaching Good for the Gospel?" *Christianity Today* 35 (October 28, 1991): 52, 54.

Litfin, A. Duane. "The Perils of Persuasive Preaching." *Christianity Today* (February 4, 1977): 14-17.

Long, Thomas G. "Preaching Apocalyptic Literature." *Review and Expositor* 90 (Summer 1993): 371-81.

Loscalzo, Craig A. "Back to the Future: Preaching into the Third Millennium." *Preaching* 7 (1992): 27-31.

McBride, Neal F. "Evangelism and Baby Boomers." *Christian Education Journal* 11 (1990): 41-49.

Marshall, I. H. "Preaching the Kingdom of God." *Expository Times* 89 (October 1977): 13-16.

Mosser, David N. "Preaching the Gospel to Those Who've Already Heard." *Preaching* 8 (July-August 1992): 18-22.

Murchison, D. Cameron, Jr. "Preaching for Conversion." *Journal for Preachers* 15 (1992): 21-25.

Roach, Patricia M. "To Evangelize the People and Redeem the Systems of the Human City." *Church and Society* 78 (September-October 1987): 20-22.

Robinson, Paul M. "Preaching for Decisions." *Brethren Life and Thought* 29 (Summer 1984): 158-63.

Schaper, Robert N. "Evangelical Preaching: A New Openness." *The Christian Ministry* 18 (September-October 1987): 18-22.

Suter, Keith D. "Evangelism in Affluent Societies." *South East Asia Journal of Theology* 21 (1980): 111-24.

Trott, Jon. "Stomping Satan with Style: How Christians Get Their Rhetorical Kicks." *Searching Together* 14 (1985): 21-25.

Weeden, Larry K. "Effective Invitations: Six Fresh Ways to Awaken People to Commitment." *Leadership* 9 (Fall 1988): 124-28.

White, James F. "The Missing Jewel of the Evangelical Church." *Reformed Journal* 36 (June 1986): 11-16.

Willimon, William H. "Preaching the Gospel in an Awkward Age." *Journal for Preachers* 15 (1992): 2-7.